APPLAUSE FIRST FOLIO EDITIONS

A Midsommer Nights Dreame

BY

William Shakespeare

PREPARED & ANNOTATED BY

NEIL FREEMAN

APPLAUSE
NEW YORK • LONDON

The Applause Shakespeare Library

Folio Texts

AN APPLAUSE ORIGINAL

A Midsommer Nights Dreame

original concept devised by Neil Freeman

original research computer entry by Margaret McBride

original software programmes designed and developed by
James McBride and Terry Lim

Text layout designed and executed by Neil Freeman

Some elements of this text were privately published under the collective title of
The Freeman–Nichols Folio Scripts 1991–96

Copyright © 1998 by Folio Scripts, Vancouver, Canada

ISBN: 1-55783-293-5

Library of Congress Cataloging-in-Publication Data

Shakespeare, William, 1564–1616.
    A Midsommer nights dreame / by William Shakespeare ; prepared &
annotated by Neil Freeman.
        p.   cm. -- (The Applause Shakespeare library. Folio texts)
        ISBN 1-55783-293-5 (pbk.)
        1. Man-woman relationships--Greece--Athens--Drama.   I. Freeman,
Neil.   II. Title.   III. Series.
PR2751.A1527   1997
822.3'3--dc21   97-9572
                                                            CIP

British Library Cataloging-in-Publication Data

A catalogue record of this book is available from the British Library

APPLAUSE BOOKS

211 West 71st Street
New York, NY 10023
Phone (212) 496-7511
Fax: (212) 721-2856

CONTENTS

ACKNOWLEDGEMENTS

My grateful thanks to all who have helped in the growth and development of this work. Special thanks to Norman Welsh who first introduced me to the Folio Text, and to Tina Packer who (with Kristin Linklater and all the members of Shakespeare & Co.) allowed me to explore the texts on the rehearsal floor. To Jane Nichols for her enormous generosity in providing the funding which allowed the material to be computerised. To James and Margaret McBride and Terry Lim for their expertise, good humour and hard work. To the National Endowment for the Arts for their award of a Major Artist Fellowship and to York University for their award of the Joseph G. Green Fellowship. To actors, directors, and dramaturgs at the Stratford Festival, Ontario; Toronto Free Theatre (that was); the Skylight Theatre, Toronto; and Tamanhouse Theatre of Vancouver. To colleagues, friends, and students at The University of British Columbia, Vancouver; York University, Toronto; Concordia University, Montreal; The National Theatre School of Canada in Montreal; Equity Showcase Theatre, Toronto; The Centre for Actors Study and Training (C.A.S.T.), Toronto; The National Voice Intensive at Simon Fraser University, Vancouver; Studio 58 of Langara College, Vancouver; Professional Workshops in the Arts, Vancouver; U.C.L.A., Los Angeles; Loyola Marymount, Los Angeles; San Jose State College, California; Long Beach State College, California; Brigham Young University, Utah and Hawaii; Holy Cross College, Massachusetts; Guilford College, North Carolina. To Chairman John Wright and Associate Dean Don Paterson for their incredible personal support and encouragement. To Rachel Ditor and Tom Scholte for their timely research assistance. To Alan and Chris Baker and Stephanie McWilliams for typographical advice. To Jay L. Halio, Hugh Richmond, and G. B. Shand for their critical input. To the overworked and underpaid proofreading teams of Ron Oten and Yuuattee Tanipersaud, Patrick Galligan and Leslie Barton, Janet Van De Graaff and Angela Dorhman (with input from Todd Sandomirsky, Bruce Alexander Pitkin, Catelyn Thornton, and Michael Roberts). And above all to my wife Julie, for her patient encouragement, courteous advice, critical eye, and long sufferance!

SPECIAL ACKNOWLEDGEMENTS

Paul Sugarman, Glenn Young, and Rachel Reiss of Applause Books; Houghton Mifflin Company for permission to quote from the line numbering system developed for *The Riverside Shakespeare*: Evans, Gwynne Blakemore, Harry Levin, Anne Barton, Herschel Baker, Frank Kermode, Hallet D. Smith, and Marie Edel, editors, *The Riverside Shakespeare*. Copyright © 1974 by Houghton Mifflin Company.

DEFINITIONS OF AND GUIDE TO PHOTOGRAPHIC COPIES OF THE EARLY TEXTS

(see Appendix A for a brief history of the First Folio, the Quartos, and their uneasy relationship with modern texts)

A QUARTO (Q)

A single text, so called because of the book size resulting from a particular method of printing. Eighteen of Shakespeare's plays were published in this format by different publishers at various dates between 1594–1622 prior to the appearance of the 1623 Folio. Of the eighteen quarto texts, scholars suggest that fourteen have value as source texts. An extremely useful collection of them is to be found in Michael J. B. Allen and Kenneth Muir, eds., *Shakespeare's Plays in Quarto* (Berkeley: University of California Press, 1981).

THE FIRST FOLIO (F1)[1]

Thirty-six of Shakespeare's plays (excluding *Pericles* and *Two Noble Kinsmen,* in which he had a hand) appeared in one volume published in 1623. All books of this size were termed Folios, again because of the sheet size and printing method, hence this volume is referred to as the First Folio; two recent photographic editions of the work are:

Charlton Hinman, ed., *The Norton Facsimile (The First Folio of Shakespeare)* (1968; republished New York: W. W. Norton & Company, Inc., 1996).

Helge Kökeritz, ed., *Mr. William Shakespeare's Comedies, Histories & Tragedies* (New Haven: Yale University Press, 1954).

THE SECOND FOLIO (F2)

Scholars suggest that the Second Folio, dated 1632 but perhaps not published until 1640, has little authority, especially since it created hundreds of new problematical readings of its own. Nevertheless, more than eight hundred modern text readings can be attributed to it. The most recent reproduction is D. S. Brewer, ed., *Mr. William Shakespeare's Comedies, Histories & Tragedies, the Second Folio Reproduced in Facsimile* (Dover, NH: Boydell & Brewer Ltd., 1985).

---

[1] For a full overview of the First Folio see the monumental two-volume work: Charlton Hinman, *The Printing and Proof Reading of the First Folio of Shakespeare* (2 volumes) (Oxford: Clarendon Press, 1963) and W. W. Greg, *The Editorial Problem in Shakespeare: a Survey of the Foundations of the Text,* 3rd. ed. (Oxford: Clarendon Press, 1954); for a brief summary, see the forty-six page publication from Peter W. M. Blayney, *The First Folio of Shakespeare* (Washington, DC: Folger Library Publications, 1991).

The Third Folio (1664) and the Fourth Folio (1685) have even less authority, and are rarely consulted except in cases of extreme difficulty.

THE THIRD FOLIO (F3)

The Third Folio, carefully proofed (though apparently not against the previous edition) takes great pains to correct anomalies in punctuation ending speeches and in expanding abbreviations. It also introduced seven new plays supposedly written by Shakespeare, only one of which, *Pericles*, has been established as such. The most recent reproduction is D. S. Brewer, ed., *Mr. William Shakespeare's Comedies, Histories & Tragedies, the Third Folio Reproduced in Facsimile* (Dover, NH: Boydell & Brewer Ltd., 1985).

THE FOURTH FOLIO (F4)

Paradoxically, while the Fourth Folio was the most carefully edited of all, its concentration on grammatical clarity and ease of comprehension by its readers at the expense of faithful reproduction of F1 renders it the least useful for those interested in the setting down on paper of Elizabethan theatre texts. The most recent reproduction is D. S. Brewer, ed., *Mr. William Shakespeare's Comedies, Histories & Tragedies, the Fourth Folio Reproduced in Facsimile* (Dover, NH: Boydell & Brewer Ltd., 1985).

WELCOME TO THESE SCRIPTS

These scripts are designed to do three things:

1. show the reader what the First Folio (often referred to as F1) set down on paper, rather than what modern editions think ought to have been set down
2. provide both reader and theatre practitioner an easy journey through some of the information the original readers might have garnered from F1 and other contemporary scripts which is still relevant today
3. provide a simple way for readers to see not only where modern texts alter the First Folio, and how, but also allow readers to explore both First Folio and modern versions of the disputed passage without having to turn to an Appendix or a different text

all this, hopefully without interfering with the action of the play.

What the First Folio sets on paper will be the basis for what you see. In the body of the play-text that follows, the words (including spellings and capitalisations), the punctuation (no matter how ungrammatical), the structure of the lines (including those moments of peculiar verse or unusual prose), the stage directions, the act and scene divisions, and (for the most part) the prefixes used for each character will be as set in the First Folio.

In addition, new, on page, visual symbols specially devised for these texts will help point out both the major stepping stones in the Elizabethan debate/rhetorical process contained in the plays (a fundamental part of understanding both the inner nature of each character as well as the emotional clashes between them), and where and how (and sometimes why) modern texts have altered the First Folio information. And, unlike any other script, opposite each page of text will be a blank page where readers can make their own notes and commentary.

However, there will be the rare occasion when these texts do not exactly follow the First Folio.

Sometimes F1's **words or phrases** are meaningless; for example, the lovely misprinting of 'which' in *Twelfth Night* as 'wh?ch', or in *Romeo and Juliet* the type-setting corruptions of 'speeh' for 'speech' and the running of the two words 'not away' as 'notaway'. If there are no alternative contemporary texts (a Quarto version of the play) or if no modification was made by any of the later Folios (The Second Folio of 1632, The Third Folio of 1664, or The Fourth Folio of 1685, termed F2, F3, and F4 respectively) then the F1 printing will be set as is, no matter how peculiar, and the modern correction footnoted. However, if a more appropriate alternative is available in a Quarto (often referred to as Q) or F2, F3, or F4, that 'correction' will be set directly into the text, replacing the F1 reading, and footnoted accordingly, as in the case of 'wh?ch', 'speeh', and 'notaway'.

The only time F1's **punctuation** will be altered is when the original setting is so blurred that an accurate deciphering of what F1 set cannot be determined. In such cases, alternative punctuation from F2–4 or Q will be set and a footnote will explain why.

The only time F1's **line structure** will not be followed is when at the end of a very long line, the final word or part of the word cannot fit onto the single line, nor be set as a new line in F1 because of the text that follows and is therefore set above or below the original line at the right hand side of the column. In such rare cases these texts will complete the line as a single line, and mark it with a † to show the change from F1. In all other cases, even when in prose F1 is forced to split the final word of a speech in half, and set only a few letters of it on a new line—for example in *Henry the Fifth*, Pistoll's name is split as 'Pi' on one line and 'stoll' (as the last part of the speech) on the next—these texts will show F1 exactly as set.

Some liberties have to be taken with the **prefixes** (the names used at the beginning of speeches to show the reader which character is now speaking), for Ff (all the Folios) and Qq (all the Quartos) are not always consistent. Sometimes slightly different abbreviations are used for the same character—in *The Tempest,* King Alonso is variously referred to as 'Al.', 'Alo.', 'Alon.', and 'Alonso'. Sometimes the same abbreviation is used for two different characters—in *A Midsummer Nights Dream* the characters Quince, the 'director' and author of the Mechanicals play, and Titania, Queen of the fairies, are given the same abbreviation 'Qu.'. While in this play common sense can distinguish what is intended, the confusions in *Julius Caesar* between Lucius and Lucullus, each referred to sometimes as 'Luc.', and in *The Comedy of Errors,* where the twin brothers Antipholus are both abbreviated to 'Antiph.', cannot be so easily sorted out. Thus, whereas F1 will show a variety of abbreviated prefixes, these texts will usually choose just one complete name per character and stay with it throughout.

However, there are certain cases where one full name will not suffice. Sometimes F1 will change the prefix for a single character from scene to scene, the change usually reflecting the character's new function or status. Thus in *The Comedy of Errors,* as a drinking companion of the local Antipholus, the goldsmith Angelo is referred to by his given name 'Ang.', but once business matters go awry he very quickly becomes a businessman, referred to as 'Gold'. Similar changes affect most of the characters in *A Midsummer Nights Dream,* and a complex example can be found in *Romeo and Juliet.* While modern texts give Juliet's mother the single prefix Lady Capulet throughout (incorrectly since neither she nor Capulet are named as aristocrats anywhere in the play) both Ff and Qq refer to her in a wonderful character-revealing multiplicity of ways—Mother, Capulet Wife, Lady, and Old Lady—a splendid gift for actress, director, designer, and reader alike.

Surprisingly, no modern text ever sets any of these variations. Believing such changes integral to the development of the characters so affected, these texts will. In such cases, each time the character's prefix changes the new prefix will be set, and a small notation alongside the prefix (either by reference to the old name, or by adding the symbol •) will remind the reader to whom it refers.

Also, some alterations will be made to F1's **stage directions,** not to the words themselves or when they occur, but to the way they are going to be presented visually. Scholars agree F1 contains two different types of stage direction: those that came in the original manuscript from which the Playhouse copy of the play was made, and a second set that were added in for theatrical clarification by the Playhouse. The scholars conjecture that the literary or manuscript directions, presumably from Shakespeare, mainly dealing with entries and key actions such as battles, are those that F1 sets centred on a separate line, while the additional Playhouse directions, usually dealing with offstage sounds, music, and exits, are those F1 sets alongside the spoken dialogue, usually flush against the right hand side of the column. In performance terms there seems to be a useful distinction between the two, though this is only a rule of thumb. The centred manuscript (Shakespearean?) directions tend to stop or change the action of the play, that is, the scene is affected by the action the direction demands, whereas the Playhouse directions (to the side of the text) serve to underscore what is already taking place. (If a word is needed to distinguish the two, the centred directions can be called 'action' directions, because they are events in and of themselves, while the side-set directions could be called 'supportive' or 'continuous' since they tend not to distract from the current onstage action.)

Since F1 seems to visually distinguish between the two types (setting them on different parts of the page) and there seems to be a logical theatrical differentiation as to both the source and function of each, it seems only appropriate that these scripts also mark the difference between them. Both Ff and Qq's side-set directions are often difficult to decipher while reading the text: sometimes they are set so close to the spoken text they get muddled up with it, despite the different typeface, and oftentimes have to be abbreviated to fit in. These are drawbacks shared by most modern texts. Thus these texts will distinguish them in a slightly different way (see p. xxvi below).

Finally, there will be two occasional alterations to Ff's **fonts.** F1 used **italics** for a large number of different purposes, sometimes creating confusion on the page. What these texts will keep as italics are letters, poems, songs, and the use of foreign languages. What they will not set in italics are real names, prefixes, and stage directions. Also at the top of each play, and sometimes at the beginning of a letter or poem, F1 would set a large wonderfully **decorative opening letter,** with the second letter of the word being capitalised, the style tying in with the borders that surrounded the opening and closing of each play. Since these texts will not be reproducing the decorative borders, the decorative letters won't be set either.

MAKING FULL USE OF THESE TEXTS

WHAT MODERN CHANGES WILL BE SHOWN

WORDS AND PHRASES

Modern texts often tidy up F1's words and phrases. Real names, both of people and places, and foreign languages are often reworked for modern understanding; for example, the French town often set in F1 as 'Callice' is usually reset as 'Calais'. Modern texts 'correct' the occasional Elizabethan practice of setting a singular noun with plural verb (and vice versa), as well as the infrequent use of the past tense of a verb to describe a current situation. These texts will set the F1 reading, and footnote the modern corrections whenever they occur.

More problematical are the possibilities of choice, especially when a Q and F version of the same play show a different reading for the same line and either choice is valid—even more so when both versions are offered by different modern texts. Juliet's 'When I shall die,/Take him and cut him out in little starres' offered by Ff/Q1-3 being offset by Q4's 'When he shall die...' is a case in point. Again, these texts will set the F1 reading, and footnote the alternatives.

LINE STRUCTURE CHANGES RELATED TO PROBLEMS OF 'CASTING-OFF'

The First Folio was usually prepared in blocks of twelve pages at a time. Six pairs of pages would be prepared, working both forward and backward simultaneously. Thus from the centre of any twelve-page block, pages six and seven were set first, then five and eight, then four and nine, then three and ten, then two and eleven, and finally one and twelve. This meant each compositor had to work out very carefully how much copy would fit not only each sheet, but also how much would be needed overall to reach the outer edges of pages one and twelve to match it to the previously set text, (prior to page one) or about to be set text (after page twelve). Naturally the calculations weren't always accurate. Sometimes there was too little text left for too great a space: in such cases, if the manuscript were set as it should have been, a great deal of empty paper would be left free, a condition often described as 'white' space. Sometimes too much text remained for too small a space, and if the manuscript were to be set according to its normal layout, every available inch would be taken up with type (and even then the text might not fit), a condition that could be described as 'crammed space'.

Essentially, this created a huge design problem, and most commentators suggest when it arose the printing house policy was to sacrifice textual accuracy to neatness of design. Thus, so the argument goes, in the case of white space, extra lines of type would have to be created where (presumably) none originally existed. *Hamlet* provides an excellent example with the Polonius speech 'Indeed that's out of the air' starting at line 78 of what most modern texts term Act Two Scene 2. Q2 sets the four-line speech as prose, and most modern texts follow suit. However, F1, faced with a potentially huge white space problem at the bottom of the right hand column of p. 261 in the Tragedy section, resets the speech as eleven lines of very irregular verse! In the case of crammed space, five lines of verse might suddenly become three lines of prose, or in one very severe case of overcrowding in *Henry The Fourth Part Two,* words, phrases, and even half lines of text might be omitted to reduce the text sufficiently.

When such cases occur, this text will set F1 as shown, and the modern texts' suggested alternatives will be footnoted and discussed.

LINE STRUCTURE CHANGES NOT RELATED TO PROBLEMS OF 'CASTING-OFF'

In addition, modern texts regularly make changes to F1's line structure which are not related to 'white' or 'crammed' space, often to the detriment of both character and scene. Two major reasons are offered for the changes.

First, either (a few) prose lines suddenly appear in what essentially is a verse scene (or a few verse lines in a sea of prose) and the modern texts, feeling the scene should be standardised, restructure the offending lines accordingly. *The Tempest* is atrociously served this way[2], for where F1, the only source text, shows the conspirators Caliban, Stephano, and, very occasionally, Trinculo, speaking verse as well as prose even within the same speech (a sure sign of personal striving and inner disturbance) most modern texts readjust the lines to show only Caliban speaking verse (dignifying him more than he deserves) and Stephano and Trinculo only speaking prose (thus robbing them of their dangerous flights of fancy).

Second, some Ff verse lines appear so appallingly defective in terms of their rhythm and length that modern texts feel it necessary to make a few 'readjustments' of the lines around them to bring the offending lines back to a coherent, rhythmic whole. Many of the later plays are abominably served in this regard: in *Macbeth,* for example, over a hundred F1 passages involving more than 200 lines (90 percent of which were set by the usually reliable compositor A) have been altered by most modern texts. Most of these changes concentrate on regularising moments where a character is under tremendous upheaval and hardly likely to be speaking pure formal verse at that particular moment!

These changes come about through a mistaken application of modern grammatical considerations to texts that were originally prepared not according to grammar

---

[2]   Commentators suggest the copy play used for setting F1, coming from Stratford as it did, and thus unsupervised by Shakespeare in the Playhouse preparation of the document, prepared by Ralph Crane, was at times defective, especially in distinguishing clearly between verse and prose: this is why most modern texts do not follow F1's choices in these dubious passages: readers are invited to explore *The Tempest* within this series, especially the footnotes, as a theatrical vindication of the original F1 setting

but rhetoric. One of rhetoric's many strengths is that it can show not only when characters are in self-control but also when they are not. In a rhetorically set passage, the splutters of a person going through an emotional breakdown, as with Othello, can be shown almost verbatim, with peculiar punctuations, spellings, breaks, and all. If the same passage were to be set grammatically it would be very difficult to show the same degree of personal disintegration on the printed page.[3] F1's occasional weird shifts between verse and prose and back again, together with the moments of extreme linear breakdown, are the equivalents of human emotional breakdown, and once the anomalies of Elizabethan script preparation are accounted for,[4] the rhetorical breakdowns on F1's printed page are clear indications of a character's disintegration within the play. When modern texts tidy up such blemishes grammatically they unwittingly remove essential theatrical and/or character clues for reader and theatre person alike.

In these texts, F1's line structure will be set as is, and all such modern alterations (prose to verse, verse to prose, regularisation of originally unmetrical lines) will be shown. The small symbol ° will be added to show where modern texts suggest a line should end rather than where F1 shows it does. A thin vertical line will be set to the left alongside any text where the modern texts have converted F1's prose to verse, or vice versa. The more large-scale of these changes will be boxed for quicker reader recognition. Most of these changes will be footnoted in the text where they occur, and a comparison of the two different versions of the text and what each could signify theatrically will be offered. For examples of both, see p. xxiii below.

THE SPECIAL PROBLEMS AFFECTING WHAT ARE KNOWN AS 'SHARED' OR 'SPLIT' VERSE LINES

A definition, and their importance to the Shakespeare texts

Essentially, split lines are short lines of verse which, when placed together, form the equivalent of a full verse line. Most commentators suggest they are very useful in speeding the play along, for the second character (whose line attaches on to the end of the first short line) is expected to use the end of the first character's line as a springboard and jump in with an immediate reply, enhancing the quickness of the debate. Thus in *Measure for Measure*, Act Two Scene 2, modern ll. 8–10, the

---

[3]   For a full discussion of this, readers are directed to Neil Freeman, *Shakespeare's First Texts* (Vancouver: Folio Scripts, 1994).

[4]   Readers are referred to an excellent chapter by Gary Taylor which analyses the whole background, conjectured and known, concerning the preparation of the first scripts. He points out the pitfalls of assuming the early texts as sole authority for all things Shakespearean: he examines the conjectured movement of the scripts from Shakespeare's pen to printed edition, and carefully examples the changes and alterations that could occur, (most notably at the hands of the manuscript copyists), as well as the interferences and revampings of the Playhouse, plus the effects of the first typesetters' personal habits and carelessness. Stanley Wells and Gary Taylor, *William Shakespeare: A Textual Companion* (Oxford: Clarendon Press, 1987), 1–68.

Provost, trying to delay Claudio's execution, has asked Angelo whether Claudio has to die the following day: Angelo's questioning affirmation ends with a very pointed short line, followed immediately by a short line opening from the Provost.

Angelo	Did I not tell thee yea? hadst thou not order?
	Why do'st thou aske againe?
Provost	Lest I might be too rash:
	Under your good correction, I have seene
	When after execution . . .

If the Provost replies immediately after, or just as, Angelo finishes, an explosive dramatic tension is created. Allowing a minor delay before reply, as many actors do, will reduce the impact of the moment, and create a hesitation where one probably does not exist.

The occasional problem

So far so good. But the problems start when more than two short lines follow each other. If there are three short lines in succession, which should be joined, #1 and #2, or #2 and #3? Later in the same scene, Claudio's sister Isabella has, at the insistence of Claudio's friend Lucio, come to plead with Angelo for her brother's life. In Lucio's eyes she is giving up too easily, hence the following (modern ll. 45–49):

Lucio	You are too cold: if you should need a pin,
	You could not with more tame a tongue desire it:
	To him, I say.
Isabella	Must he needs die?
Angelo	Maiden, no remedie?

And here it seems fairly obvious Isabella and Angelo's lines should join together, thus allowing a wonderful dramatic pause following Lucio's urging before Isabella plucks up enough courage to try. Most modern texts set the lines accordingly, with Lucio's the short odd line out.

But what about the three lines contained in the exchange that follows almost straightaway?

Isabella	But you might doe't & do the world no wrong
	If so your heart were touch'd with that remorse,
	As mine is to him?
Angelo	Hee's sentenc'd, tis too late.
Lucio	You are too cold.
Isabella	Too late? why no: I that doe speak a word
	May call it againe: well, beleeve this
	(modern line numbering 53–56)

Does Angelo's 'Hee's sentenc'd...' spring off Isabella's line, leaving Isabella speechless and turning to go before Lucio urges her on again? Or does Angelo pause (to frame a reply?) before speaking, leaving Lucio to quickly jump in quietly giving Isabella no time to back off? Either choice is possible, and dramatically valid. And readers should be allowed to make their own choice, which automatically means each reader should able to see the possibility of such choices when they occur.

The problem magnified by the way modern texts set split/shared lines

However, because of a peculiarity faced by the modern texts not shared by Ff/Qq, modern texts rarely show such possibilities to their readers but make the choice for them. The peculiarity comes about from a change in text layout initiated in the eighteenth century.

Ff/Qq always set short lines directly under one another, as shown in the examples above. In 1778 George Steevens, a highly respected editor, started to show split lines a new way, by advancing the second split line to just beyond where the first split line finishes, viz.

Angelo	Did I not tell thee yea? hadst thou not order?
	Why do'st thou aske againe?
Provost	Lest I might be too rash:
	Under your good correction, I have seene
	When after execution...

Since that date all editions of Shakespeare have followed this practice, which is fine as long as there are only two short lines, but when three follow each other, a choice has to be made. Thus the second Isabella/Angelo/Lucio sequence could be set as either

Isabella	But you might doe't & do the world no wrong
	If so your heart were touch'd with that remorse,
	As mine is to him?
Angelo	Hee's sentenc'd, tis too late.
Lucio	You are too cold.
Isabella	Too late? why no: I that doe speak a word
	May call it againe: well, beleeve this...

(the usual modern choice), or

Isabella	But you might doe't & do the world no wrong
	If so your heart were touch'd with that remorse,
	As mine is to him?
Angelo	Hee's sentenc'd, tis too late.
Lucio	You are too cold.

Isabella	Too late? why no: I that doe speak a word
	May call it againe: well, beleeve this . . .

This modern typesetting convention has robbed the reader of a very important moment of choice. Indeed, at the beginning of the twentieth century, Richard Flatter[5] suggested that what modern commentators consider to be split lines may not be split lines at all. He offers two other suggestions: pauses and hesitations could exist between each line, or the lines could in fact be spoken one on top of another, a very important consideration for the crowd responses to Anthony in the funeral scene of *Julius Caesar*. Either way, the universally adopted Steevens layout precludes the reader/theatre practitioner from even seeing such possibilities.

These texts will show the F1 layout as is, and will indicate via footnote when a choice is possible (in the case of three short lines, or more, in succession) and by the symbol } when the possibility of springboarding exists. Thus the Folio Texts would show the first Angelo/Provost example as:

Angelo	Did I not tell thee yea? hadst thou not order?
	Why do'st thou aske againe?
	}
Provost	Lest I might be too rash:
	Under your good correction, I have seene
	When after execution . . .

In nearly all cases the } shows where most modern texts insist on setting a shared split line. However, readers are cautioned that in many of the later plays, the single line so created is much longer than pentameter, and often very a-rhythmic. In such cases the lines could have great value as originally set (two separate short lines), especially when a key debate is in process (for example, *Measure for Measure, The Tragedie of Cymbeline, Othello,* and *The Winters Tale*).

THE UNUSUAL SINGLE SPLIT LINE (PLEASE SEE 'A CAVEAT', P. XXXVIII)

So far the discussion has centred on short lines shared by two or more characters. Ff/Qq offer another complication rarely, if ever, accepted by most modern texts. Quite often, and not because of white space, a single character will be given two consecutive short lines within a single speech. *Romeo and Juliet* is chock full of this device: in the famous balcony scene (modern texts numbering 2.2.62–3) Juliet asks Romeo

How cam'st thou hither.
Tell me, and wherefore?
The Orchard walls are high, and hard to climbe

The first two lines (five syllables each) suggest a minute pause between them as Juliet hesitates before asking the all important second line (with its key second part

---

5   Richard Flatter, *Shakespeare's Producing Hand* (London: Heinemann, 1948, reprint).

'and wherefore'). Since Qq rarely set such 'single split lines' most modern texts refuse to set any of them, but combine them:

> How cams't thou hither. Tell me and wherefore?

This basically F1 device is set by all the compositors and followed by all other Folios. This text will follow suit, highlighting them with the symbol → for quick recognition, viz.:

> How cam'st thou hither. →
> Tell me, and wherefore?
> The Orchard walls are high, and hard to climbe

SENTENCE AND PUNCTUATION STRUCTURES

A CHARACTER'S THOUGHTFUL & EMOTIONAL JOURNEY

A quick comparison between these texts and both the Ff/Qq's and the modern texts will reveal two key differences in the layout of the dialogue on the printed page — the bolding of major punctuation, and the single line dropping of text whenever a new sentence begins.

The underlying principle behind these texts is that since the handwritten documents from which they stem were originally intended for the actor and Playhouse, in addition to their poetical values, the Ff/Qq scripts represent a theatrical process. Even if the scripts are being read just for pleasure, at the back of the reader's mind should be the notion of characters on a stage and actors acting (and the word 'process' rather than 'practice' is deliberate, with process suggesting a progression, development, or journey).

The late Jean-Louis Barrault gave a wonderful definition of acting, and of this journey, suggesting an actor's job was to strive to remain in 'the ever-changing present'. If something happens onstage (an entry, an exit, a verbal acceptance or denial of what the actor's character has suggested), the 'present' has changed, and the character must readjust accordingly. Just as onstage, the actor should be prepared for the character to re-adjust, and in rehearsal should be examining how and why it does, so should the reader in the library, armchair, or classroom.

In many ways, the key to Shakespeare is discovering how each character's mind works; perceiving the emotions and intellects as they act and react helps the reader understand from where the poetical imagination and utterance stem.

Certain elements of each character's emotional and intellectual journey, and where it changes, are encoded into the sentence structure of Ff/Qq.

Elizabethan education prepared any schooled individual (via the 'petty school' and the private tutor) for the all important and essential daily rough and tumble of argument and debate. Children were trained not only how to frame an argument so as to win it hands down, but also how to make it entertaining so as to enthrall the neutral listener.

The overall training, known as 'rhetoric', essentially allowed intellect and emotion to exist side by side, encouraging the intellect to keep the emotion in check. The idea was not to deny the emotions, but ensure they didn't swamp the 'divinity' of reason, the only thing separating man from beast. While the initial training was mainly vocal, any written matter of the period automatically reflected the ebb and flow of debate. What was set on the printed page was not grammar, but a representation of the rhetorical process.

DROPPING A LINE TO ILLUSTRATE F1'S SENTENCE STRUCTURE

Put at its simplest, in any document of the period, each sentence would represent a new intellectual and emotional stage of a rhetorical argument. When this stage of the argument was completed, a period would be set (occasionally a question mark or, much more rarely, an exclamation mark—both followed by a capital letter) signifying the end of that stage of the argument, and the beginning of the next.

Thus in the First Folio, the identification of each new sentence is an automatic (and for us, four hundred years later, a wonderful) aid to understanding how a character is reacting to and dealing with Barrault's ever-changing present.

To help the reader quickly spot the new steppingstone in an argument, and thus the point of transition, these texts highlight where one sentence ends and the new one begins by simply dropping a line whenever a new sentence starts. Thus the reader has a visual reminder that the character is making a transition to deal with a change in the current circumstances of the scene (or in the process of self-discovery in the case of soliloquies).

This device has several advantages. The reader can instantly see where the next step in the argument begins. The patterns so created on the page can quickly illuminate whenever a contrast between characters' thought patterns occurs. (Sometimes the sentences are short and precise, suggesting the character is moving quickly from one idea to the next. Sometimes the sentences are very long, suggesting the character is undergoing a very convoluted process. Sometimes the sentences contain nothing but facts, suggesting the character has no time to entertain; sometimes they are filled with high-flown imagery, perhaps suggesting the character is trying to mask a very weak argument with verbal flummery.) The patterns can also show when a character's style changes within itself, say from long and convoluted to short and precise, or vice versa. It can also immediately pinpoint when a character is in trouble and not arguing coherently or logically, something modern texts often alter out of grammatical necessity.

With patience, all this could be gleaned from the modern texts (in as far as they set the Ff sentence structure, which they often don't) and from a photostat of the First Folio, by paying special attention to where the periods are set. But there is one extra very special advantage to this new device of dropping a line: this has to do once more with the Elizabethan method of setting down spoken argument on paper, especially when the character speaking is not in the best of all possible worlds.

If an Elizabethan person/character is arguing well, neatly, cleanly, tidily, then a printed representation of that argument would also be clean, neat, and tidy — to modern eyes it would be grammatically acceptable. If the same character is emotionally upset, or incapable of making a clear and tidy argument, then the on-paper representation would be muddy and untidy — to modern eyes totally ungrammatical and often not acceptable. By slightly isolating each sentence these texts very quickly allow the reader to spot when a sentence's construction is not all that it should be, say in the middle of Viola's so-called ring speech in *Twelfth Night* (Act Two Scene 2), or Helena's declaration of love for Bertram in *All's Well That Ends Well* (Act One Scene 3), or the amazing opening to *As You Like It,* where Orlando's opening litany of complaint against his brother starts with a single sentence twenty lines long.

This is especially relevant when a surprising modern editorial practice is accounted for. Very often the Ff sentence structures are markedly altered by modern texts, especially when the Ff sentences do not seem 'grammatical' — thus Orlando's twenty-line monster is split into six separate, grammatically correct sentences by all modern texts. And then there is the case of Shylock in *The Merchant of Venice,* a Jewish man being goaded and tormented beyond belief by the very Christians who helped his daughter elope with a Christian, taking a large part of Shylock's fortune with her. A sentence comparison of the famous Act Three Scene 1 speech culminating in 'Hath not a Jew eyes?' is very instructive. All modern texts set the speech as between fifteen and seventeen sentences in length: whatever the pain, anger, and personal passion, the modern texts encourage dignity and self-control, a rational Shylock. But this is a Shylock completely foreign to both Q1 and Ff. Q1 show the same speech as only four sentences long, Ff five — a veritable onflow of intellect and passion all mixed together, all unstoppable for the longest period of time — a totally different being from that shown by the modern texts. What is more, this is a totally different Shylock from the one seen earlier in the Ff/Q1 version of the play, where, even in the extremes of discomfort with the old enemy Anthonio, his sentence structures are rhetorically balanced and still grammatical to modern eyes.

Here, with Shylock, there are at least three benefits to dropping the sentence: the unusualness of the speech is immediately spotted; the change in style between this and any of his previous speeches can be quickly seen; and, above all, the moment where the speech moves from a long unchecked outpouring to a quick series of brief, dangerously rational sentences can be quickly identified. And these advantages will be seen in such changed sentence circumstances in any play in any of these texts.

THE HIGHLIGHTING OF THE MAJOR PUNCTUATION IN THESE TEXTS

A second key element of rhetoric encoded into the Ff/Qq texts clearly shows the characters' mind in action. The encoding lies in the remaining punctuation which, unlike much modern punctuation, serves a double function, one dealing with the formation of the thought, the other with the speaking of it.

Apart from the period, dealt with already, essentially there are two sets of punctuation to consider, minor and major, each with their own very specific functions.

Shakespearean characters reflect the mode of thinking of their time. Elizabethans were trained to constantly add to or modify thoughts. They added a thought to expand the one already made. They denied the first thought so as to set up alternatives. They elaborated a thought so as to clarify what has already been said. They suddenly moved into splendid puns or non-sequiturs (emotional, logical, or both) because they had been immediately stimulated by what they or others had just said. The **minor punctuation** (essentially the comma [,] the parenthesis or bracket [( )], and the dash) reflects all this.

In establishing thought processes for each character, minor punctuation shows every new nuance of thought: every tiny punctuation in this category helps establish the deftness and dance of each character's mind. In *As You Like It* (Act Three Scene 2, modern line numbering 400–402) the Ff setting of Rosalind's playing with her beloved Orlando has a wonderful coltish exuberance as she runs rings round his protestations of love:

> Love is meerely a madnesse, and I tel you,
> deserves as well a darke house,* and a whip,* as madmen do:

Her mind is adding extra thoughts as she goes: the Ff commas are as much part of her spirit and character as the words are—though most modern texts create a much more direct essayist, preaching what she already knows, by removing the two Ff commas marked *.[6]

A similar situation exists with Macbeth, facing Duncan whom he must kill if he is to become king (Act One Scene 4, modern line numbering 22–27). Ff show a Macbeth almost swamped with extra thoughts as he assures Duncan

> The service,* and the loyaltie I owe,
> In doing it,* payes it selfe.
> Your highnesse part,* is to receive our Duties,

---

[6] Unfortunately, many modern texts eradicate the F and Q minor punctuation arguing the need for light (or infrequent) punctuation to preserve the speed of speech. This is not necessarily helpful, since what it removes is just a new thought marker, not an automatic indication to pause: too often the result is that what the first texts offer a character as a series of closely-worked out dancing thought-patterns (building one quick thought—as marked by a comma—on top of another) is turned into a series of much longer phrases: often, involved and reactive busy minds are artificially turned into (at best) eloquent ones, suddenly capable of perfect and lengthy rationality where the situation does not warrant such a reaction, or (at worst) vapid ones, speaking an almost preconceived essay of commentary or artificial sentimentality.

> And our Duties are to your Throne,* and State,
> Children,* and Servants; which doe but what they should,*
> By doing every thing safe toward your Love
> And Honour.

The heavy use of minor punctuation—especially when compared with most modern texts which remove the commas marked *, leaving Macbeth with just six thoughts compared to Ff's twelve—clearly shows a man ill at ease and/or working too hard to say the right thing. Again the punctuation helps create an understanding of the character.

However, while the minor punctuation is extremely important in the discovery process of reading and/or rehearsal, paradoxically, it mustn't become too dominant. From the performance/speaking viewpoint, to pause at each comma would be tantamount to disaster. There would be an enormous dampening effect if reader/actor were to pause at every single piece of punctuation: the poetry would be destroyed and the event would become interminable.

In many ways, minor punctuation is the Victorian child of Shakespearean texts, it must be seen but not heard. (In speaking the text, the new thought the minor punctuation represents can be added without pausing: a change in timbre, rhythm, or pitch—in acting terms, occurring naturally with changes in intention—will do the trick.)

But once thoughts have been discovered, they have to be organised into some form of coherent whole. If the period shows the end of one world and the start of the new, and if the comma marks a series of small, ever-changing, ever-evolving thoughts within each world, occasionally there must be pause for reflection somewhere in the helter-skelter of tumbling new ideas. This is the **major punctuation's** strength; major punctuation consisting of the semicolon [;], and the colon [:].

Major punctuation marks the gathering together of a series of small thoughts within an overall idea before moving onto something new. If a room full of Rodin sculptures were analogous to an Elizabethan scene or act, each individual piece of sculpture would be a speech, the torso or back or each major limb a separate sentence. Each collective body part (a hand, the wrist, the forearm, the upper arm) would be a series of small thoughts bounded by major punctuation, each smaller item within that part (a finger, a fingernail, a knuckle) a single small thought separated by commas. In describing the sculpture to a friend one might move from the smaller details (the knuckle) to the larger (the hand) to another larger (the wrist) then another (the forearm) and so on to the whole limb. Unless the speaker is emotionally moved by the recollection, some pauses would be essential, certainly after finishing the whole description of the arm (the sentence), and probably after each major collective of the hand, the wrist, etc. (as marked by the major punctuation), but not after every small bit.

As a rule of thumb, and simply stated, the colon and semicolon mark both a thinking and a speaking pause. The vital difference between major and minor punctuation, whether in the silent reading of the text or the performing of it aloud, is you need not pause at the comma, bracket, or dash; you probably should at the colon, semicolon, and period.

Why the Major Punctuation is Bolded in These Texts.

In speaking the text or reading it, the minor punctuation indicates the need to key onto the new thought without necessarily requiring a pause. In so doing, the inherent rhythms of speech, scene, and play can clip along at the rate suggested by the Prologue in *Romeo and Juliet,* 'the two hours traffic of the stage', until a pause is absolutely necessary. Leave the commas alone, and the necessary pauses will make themselves known.

The 'major' punctuation then comes into its own, demanding double attention as both a thinking and speaking device. This is why it is bolded, to highlight it for the reader's easier access. The reader can still use all the punctuation when desired, working through the speech thought by thought, taking into account both major and minor punctuation as normal. Then, when needed, the bolding of the major punctuation will allow the reader easy access for marking where the speech, scene, or play needs to be broken down into its larger thinking/speaking (and even breathing) units without affecting its overall flow.

The Blank Pages Within the Text

In each text within this series, once readers reach the play itself they will find that with each pair of pages the dialogue is printed on the right-hand page only. The left-hand page has been deliberately left blank so that readers, actors, directors, stage managers, teachers, etc. have ample space for whatever notes and text emendations they may wish to add.

PRACTICAL ON-PAGE HELP FOR THE READER

THE VISUAL SYMBOLS HIGHLIGHTING MODERN ALTERATIONS

THE BOX

This surrounds a passage where the modern texts have made whole-scale alterations to the Ff text. Each boxed section will be footnoted, and the changes analysed at the bottom of the page.

THE FOOTNOTES

With many modern texts the footnotes are not easily accessible. Often no indication is given within the text itself where the problem/choice/correction exists. Readers are forced into a rather cumbersome four-step process. First, they have to search through the bottom of the page where the footnotes are crammed together, often in very small print, to find a line number where an alteration has been made. Then they must read the note to find out what has been altered. Then they must go back to the text and search the side of the page to find the corresponding line number. Having done all this, finally they can search the line to find the word or phrase that has been changed (sometimes complicated by the fact the word in question is set twice in different parts of the line).

These texts will provide a reference marker within the text itself, directly alongside the word or phrase that is in question. This guides the reader directly to the corresponding number in the footnote section of the bottom of each page, to the alteration under discussion — hopefully a much quicker and more immediate process.

In addition, since there are anywhere between 300 and 1,100 footnotes in any one of these texts, a tool is offered to help the reader find only those notes they require, when they require them. In the footnote section, prior to the number that matches the footnote marker in the text, a letter or combination of letters will be set as a code. The letter 'W', for example, shows that the accompanying footnote refers to word substitutions offered by modern texts; the letters 'SD' refer to an added or altered stage direction; the letters 'LS' show the footnote deals with a passage where the modern texts have completely altered the line-structure that F1 set. This enables readers to be selective when they want to examine only certain changes, for they can quickly skim through the body of footnotes until they find the code they want, perhaps those dealing with changes in prefixes (the code 'P') or when modern alterations have been swapping lines from verse to prose or vice versa (the code 'VP'). For full details of the codes, see pp. xxxiii–xxxv below.

Readers are urged to make full use of the footnotes in any of the Recommended Texts listed just before the start of the play. They are excellent in their areas of expertise. To attempt to rival or paraphrase them would be redundant. Thus the footnotes in these scripts will hardly ever deal with word meanings and derivations; social or political history; literary derivations and comparisons; or lengthy quotations from scholars or commentators. Such information is readily available in the *Oxford English Dictionary* and from the recommended modern texts.

Generally, the footnotes in these scripts will deal with matters theatrical and textual and will be confined to three major areas: noting where and how the modern texts alter F1's line structure; showing popular alternative word readings often selected by the modern texts (these scripts will keep the F1 reading unless otherwise noted); and showing the rare occasions where and how these scripts deviate from their source texts. When the modern texts offer alternative words and/or phrases to F2-4/Qq, the original spelling and punctuation will be used. Where appropriate, the footnotes will briefly refer to the excellent research of the scholars of the last three centuries, and to possible theatrical reasons for maintaining F1's structural 'irregularities'.

THE SYMBOL °

This will be used to show where modern texts have altered F1's line structure, and will allow the reader to explore both the F1 setting and the modern alternative while examining the speech where it is set, in its proper context and rightful position within the play. For example, though F1 is usually the source text for *Henry the Fifth* and sets the dialogue for Pistoll in prose, most modern texts use the memorial Q version and change his lines to (at times extraordinarily peculiar) verse. These texts will set the speech as shown in F1, but add the ° to show the modern texts alterations, thus:

> Pistoll   Fortune is Bardolphs foe, and frownes on him:°
> for he hath stolne a Pax, and hanged must a be:° a damned
> death:° let Gallowes gape for Dogge, let Man goe free,°
> and let not Hempe his Wind-pipe suffocate:° but Exeter
> hath given the doome of death,° for Pax of little price.°
>
> Therefore goe speake,° the Duke will heare thy voyce;°
> and let not Bardolphs vitall thred bee cut° with edge of
> Penny-Cord, and vile reproach.°
>   Speake Captaine for
> his Life, and I will thee requite.°
>   (*Henry V*, These Scripts, 2.1.450–459)

Read the speech utilising the ° to mark the end of a line, and the reader is exploring what the modern texts suggest should be the structure. Read the lines ignoring the ° and the reader is exploring what the F1 text really is. Thus both F1 and modern/Q versions can be read within the body of the text.

THE VERTICAL LINE TO THE LEFT OF THE TEXT

This will be used to mark a passage where modern editors have altered F1's verse to prose or vice versa. Here is a passage in a predominantly prose scene from *Henry V*. Modern texts and F1 agree that Williams and Fluellen should be set in prose. However, the F1 setting for Henry could be in verse, though most modern texts set it in prose too. The thin vertical line to the left of the text is a quick reminder to the reader of disagreement between Ff and modern texts (the F1 setting will always be shown, and the disputed section will be footnoted accordingly).

> | King Henry | Twas I indeed thou promised'st to strike,
> | | And thou hast given me most bitter termes.
> | Fluellen | And please your Majestie, let his Neck answere
> | | for it, if there is any Marshall Law in the World.
> | King Henry | How canst thou make me satisfaction?
> | Williams | All offences, my Lord, come from the heart: ne-
> | | ver came any from mine, that might offend your Ma-
> | | jestie. (Henry V, These Scripts, 4.1.240-247)

THE SYMBOL } SET TO THE RIGHT OF TEXT, CONNECTING TWO SPEECHES

This will be used to remind readers of the presence of what most modern texts consider to be split or shared lines, and that therefore the second speech could springboard quickly off the first, thus increasing the speed of the dialogue and debate; for example:

> | Angelo | Did I not tell thee yea? hadst thou not order?
> | | Why do'st thou aske againe?
> | | }
> | Provost | Lest I might be too rash:
> | | Under your good correction, I have seene
> | | When after execution . . .

Since there is no definitive way of determining whether Shakespeare wished the two short lines to be used as a shared or split line, or used as two separate short lines, the reader would do well to explore the moment twice. The first time the second speech could be 'springboarded' off the first as if it were a definite shared line; the second time round a tiny break could be inserted before speaking the second speech, as if a hesitation were deliberately intended. This way both possibilities of the text can be examined.

THE SYMBOL → TO THE RIGHT OF THE TEXT, JOINING TWO SHORT LINES SPOKEN BY A SINGLE CHARACTER

This indicates that though Ff has set two short lines for a single character, perhaps hinting at a minute break between the two thoughts, most modern texts have set the two short lines as one longer one. Thus the first two lines of Juliet's

> How cam'st thou hither. →

Tell me, and wherefore?
The Orchard walls are high, and hard to climbe

can be explored as one complete line (the interpretation of most modern texts), or, as F1 suggests, as two separate thoughts with a tiny hesitation between them. In most cases these lines will be footnoted, and possible reasons for the F1 interpretation explored.

THE OCCASIONAL USE OF THE †

This marks where F1 has been forced, in a crowded line, to set the end of the line immediately above or below the first line, flush to the right hand column. These texts will set the original as one complete line—the only instance where these scripts do not faithfully reproduce F1's line structure.

THE OCCASIONAL USE OF THE † TOGETHER WITH A FOOTNOTE (ALSO SEE P. XXXVII)

This marks where a presumed F1 compositorial mistake has led to a meaningless word being set (for example 'speeh' instead of 'speech') and, since there is a 'correct' form of the word offered by either F2–4 or Qq, the correct form of the word rather than the F1 error has been set. The footnote directs the reader to the original F1 setting reproduced at the bottom of the page.

PATTERNED BRACKETS { } SURROUNDING A PREFIX OR PART OF A STAGE DIRECTION

These will be used on the infrequent occasions where a minor alteration or addition has been made to the original F1 setting.

THE VARIED USE OF THE * AND ∞

This will change from text to text. Sometimes (as in *Hamlet*) an * will be used to show where, because of the 1606 Acte To Restraine The Abuses of Players, F1 had to alter Qq's 'God' to 'Heaven'. In other plays it may be used to show the substitution of the archaic 'a' for 'he' while in others the * and /or the ∞ may be used to denote a line from Qq or F2–4 which F1 omits.

THE SYMBOL •

This is a reminder that a character with several prefixes has returned to one previously used in the play.

THE VISUAL SYMBOLS HIGHLIGHTING KEY ITEMS WITHIN THE FIRST FOLIO

THE DROPPING OF THE TEXT A SINGLE LINE

This indicates where one sentence ends, and a new one begins (see pp. xvii–xviii).

THE BOLDING OF PUNCTUATION

This indicates the presence of the major punctuation (see pp. xviii–xxi).

UNBRACKETED STAGE DIRECTIONS

These are the ones presumed to come from the manuscript copy closest to Shakespeare's own hand (F1 sets them centred, on a separate line). They usually have a direct effect on the scene, altering what has been taking place immediately prior to its setting (see p. ix).

BRACKETED STAGE DIRECTIONS

These are the ones presumed to have been added by the Playhouse. (F1 sets them alongside the dialogue, flush to the right of the column.) They usually support, rather than alter, the onstage action (see p. ix).

(The visual difference in the two sets of directions can quickly point the reader to an unexpected aspect of an entry or exit. Occasionally an entry is set alongside the text, rather than on a separate line. This might suggest the character enters not wishing to draw attention to itself, for example, towards the end of *Macbeth,* the servant entering with the dreadful news of the moving Byrnane Wood. Again, F1 occasionally sets an exit on a separate line, perhaps stopping the onstage action altogether, as with the triumphal exit to a 'Gossips feast' at the end of *The Comedy of Errors* made by most of the reunited and/or business pacified characters, leaving the servant Dromio twins onstage to finish off the play. A footnote will be added when these unusual variations in F1's directions occur.)

As with all current texts, the final period of any bracketed or unbracketed stage direction will not be set.

ACT, SCENE, AND LINE NUMBERING SPECIFIC TO THIS TEXT

Each of these scripts will show the act and scene division from F1. They will also indicate modern act and scene division, which often differs from Ff/Qq. Modern texts suggest that in many plays full scene division was not attempted until the eighteenth century, and act division in the early texts was sometimes haphazard at best. Thus many modern texts place the act division at a point other than that set in Ff/Qq, and nearly always break Ff/Qq text up into extra scenes. When modern texts add an act or scene division which is not shared by F1, the addition will be shown in brackets within the body of each individual play as it occurs. When Ff set a new Act or scene, for clarity these texts will start a fresh page, even though this is not Ff/Qq practice

ON THE LEFT HAND SIDE OF EACH PAGE

Down the left of each page, line numbers are shown in increments of five. These refer to the lines in this text only. Where F1 prints a line containing two sentences, since these scripts set two separate lines, each line will be numbered independently.

ON THE TOP RIGHT OF EACH PAGE

These numbers represent the first and last lines set on the page, and so summarise the information set down the left hand side of the text.

AT THE BOTTOM RIGHT OF EACH PAGE: USING THESE SCRIPTS WITH OTHER TEXTS

At times a reader may want to compare these texts with either the original First Folio, or a reputable modern text, or both. Specially devised line numbers will make this a fairly easy proposition. These new reference numbers will be found at the bottom right of the page, just above the footnote section.

The information before the colon allows the reader to compare these texts against any photographic reproduction of the First Folio. The information after the colon allows the reader to compare these texts with a modern text, specifically the excellent *Riverside Shakespeare*.[7]

Before the colon: any photostat of the First Folio

A capital letter plus a set of numbers will be shown followed by a lowercase letter. The numbers refer the reader to a particular page within the First Folio; the capital letter before the numbers specifies whether the reader should be looking at the right hand column (R) or left hand column (L) on that particular page; the lower case letter after the numbers indicates which compositor (mainly 'a' through 'e') set that particular column. An occasional asterisk alongside the reference tells the reader that though this is the page number as set in F1, it is in fact numbered out of sequence, and care is needed to ensure, say in *Cymbeline,* the appropriate one of two 'p. 389s' is being consulted.

Since the First Folio was printed in three separate sections (the first containing the Comedies, the second the Histories, and the third the Tragedies),[8] the pages and section in which each of these scripts is to be found will be mentioned in the introduction accompanying each play. The page number refers to that printed at the top of the reproduced Folio page, and not to the number that appears at the bottom of the page of the book which contains the reproduction.

Thus, from this series of texts, page one of *Measure for Measure* shows the reference 'L61–c'. This tells the reader that the text was set by compositor 'c' and can

---

[7]   Gwynne Blakemore Evans, Harry Levin, Anne Barton, Herschel Baker, Frank Kermode, Hallet D. Smith, and Marie Edel, eds., *The Riverside Shakespeare* (Copyright © 1974 by Houghton Mifflin Company). This work is chosen for its exemplary scholarship, editing principles, and footnotes.

[8]   The plays known as Romances were not printed as a separate section: *Cymbeline* was set with the Tragedies, *The Winter's Tale* and *The Tempest* were set within the Comedies, and though *Pericles* had been set in Q it did not appear in the compendium until F3. *Troilus and Cressida* was not assigned to any section, but was inserted between the Histories and the Tragedies with only 2 of its 28 pages numbered.

be checked against the left hand column of p. 61 of the First Folio (*Measure For Measure* being set in the Comedy Section of F1).

Occasionally the first part of the reference seen at the bottom of the page will also be seen within the text, somewhere on the right hand side of the page. This shows the reader exactly where this column has ended and the new one begins.

(As any photostat of the First Folio clearly shows, there are often sixty-five lines or more per column, sometimes crowded very close together. The late Professor Charlton Hinman employed a brilliantly simple line-numbering system (known as TLN, short for Through Line Numbering System) whereby readers could quickly be directed to any particular line within any column on any page.

The current holders of the rights to the TLN withheld permission for the system to be used in conjunction with this series of Folio Texts.)

After the colon: *The Riverside Shakespeare*

Numbers will be printed indicating the act, scene, and line numbers in *The Riverside Shakespeare,* which contain the information set on the particular page of this script. Again, using the first page of *Measure For Measure*, the reference 1.1.1–21 on page one of these scripts directs the reader to Act One Scene 1 of *The Riverside Shakespeare*; line one in *The Riverside Shakespeare* matches the first line in this text, while the last line of dialogue on page one of this text is to be found in line twenty-one of the *Riverside* version of the play.

COMMON TYPESETTING PECULIARITIES
OF THE FOLIO AND QUARTO TEXTS
(And How These Texts Present Them)

There are a few (to modern eyes) unusual contemporary Elizabethan and early Jacobean printing practices which will be retained in these scripts.

THE ABBREVIATIONS, 'S.', 'L.', 'D.', 'M.'

Ff and Qq use standard printing abbreviations when there is not enough space on a single line to fit in all the words. The most recognisable to modern eyes includes 'S.' for Saint; 'L.' for Lord; 'M.' for Mister (though this can also be short for 'Master', 'Monsieur', and on occasions even 'Mistress'); and 'D.' for Duke. These scripts will set F1 and footnote accordingly.

'Ÿ', 'W', AND ACCENTED FINAL VOWELS

Ff/Qq's two most commonly used abbreviations are not current today, viz.:

ÿ, which is usually shorthand for either 'you'; 'thee'; 'thou'; 'thy'; 'thine'; or 'yours'

w, usually with a ¨ above, shorthand for either 'which'; 'what'; 'when'; or 'where'. Also, in other cases of line overcrowding, the last letter of a relatively unimportant word is omitted, and an accent placed over the preceding vowel as a marker, e.g. 'thä' for 'than'. For all such abbreviations these scripts will set F1 and footnote accordingly.

THE SPECIAL CASE OF THE QUESTION AND EXCLAMATION MARKS
('?' AND '!')

USAGE

Elizabethan use of these marks differs somewhat from modern practice. Ff/Qq rarely set an exclamation mark: instead the question mark was used either both as a question mark and as an exclamation point. Thus occasionally the question mark suggests some minor emphasis in the reading.

SENTENCE COUNT

When either mark occurs in the middle of a speech, it can be followed by a capitalised or a lowercase word. When the word is lowercase (not capitalised) the sentence continues on without a break. The opposite is not always true: just because the following word is capitalised does not automatically signify the start of a new sentence, though more often than not it does.

Elizabethan rhetorical writing style allowed for words to be capitalised within a sentence, a practice continued by the F1 compositors. Several times in *The Winters Tale,* highly emotional speeches are set full of question marks followed by capitalised words. Each speech could be either one long sentence of ongoing passionate rush, or up to seven shorter sentences attempting to establish self-control.

The final choice belongs to the individual reader, and in cases where such alternatives arise, the passages will be boxed, footnoted, and the various possibilities discussed.

THE ENDING OF SPEECHES WITH NO PUNCTUATION, OR PUNCTUATION OTHER THAN A PERIOD

Quite often F1–2 will not show punctuation at the end of a speech, or sometimes set a colon (:) or a comma (,) instead. Some commentators suggest the setting of anything other than a period was due to compositor carelessness, and that omission occurred either for the same reason, or because the text was so full it came flush to the right hand side of the column and there was no room left for the final punctuation to be set. Thus modern texts nearly always end a speech with the standard period (.), question mark (?), or exclamation mark (!), no matter what F1–2 have set.

However, omission doesn't always occur when a line is full, and F2, though making over sixteen hundred unauthorised typographical corrections of F1 (more than eight hundred of which are accepted by most modern texts), rarely replaces an offending comma or colon with a period, or adds missing periods — F3 is the first to make such alterations on a large scale basis. A few commentators, while acknowledging some of the omissions/mistakes are likely to be due to compositor or scribal error, suggest that ending the speech with anything other than a period (or not ending the speech at all) might indicate that the character with the speech immediately following is in fact interrupting this first speaker.

These texts will set F1, footnote accordingly, and sometimes discuss the possible effect of the missing or 'incorrect' punctuation.

THE SUBSTITUTIONS OF 'i/I' FOR 'j/J' AND 'u' FOR 'v'

In both Ff/Qq words now spelled as 'Jove' or 'Joan' are often set as 'Iove' or 'Ioan'. To avoid confusion, these texts will set the modern version of the word. Similarly, words with 'v' in the middle are often set by Ff/Qq with a 'u'; thus the modern word 'avoid' becomes 'auoid'. Again, these texts will set the modern version of the word, without footnote acknowledgement.

ALTERNATIVE SETTINGS OF A WORD WHERE DIFFERENT SPELLINGS MAINTAIN THE SAME MEANING

Ff/Qq occasionally set, what appears to modern eyes, an archaic spelling of a word for which there is a more common modern alternative, for example 'murther' for murder, 'burthen' for burden, 'moe' for more, 'vilde' for vile. Some modern texts set the Ff / Qq spelling, some modernise. These texts will set the F1 spelling through-out.

ALTERNATIVE SETTINGS OF A WORD WHERE DIFFERENT SPELLINGS SUGGEST DIFFERENT MEANINGS

Far more complicated is the situation where, while an Elizabethan could substi-tute one word formation for another and still imply the same thing, to modern eyes the substituted word has a entirely different meaning to the one it has replaced. The following is by no means an exclusive list of the more common dual-spelling, dual-meaning words

anticke–antique	mad–made	sprite–spirit
born–borne	metal–mettle	sun–sonne
hart–heart	mote–moth	travel–travaill
human–humane	pour–(powre)–power	through–thorough
lest–least	reverent–reverend	troth–truth
lose–loose	right–rite	whether–whither

Some of these doubles offer a metrical problem too; for example 'sprite', a one syllable word, versus 'spirit'. A potential problem occurs in *A Midsummer Nights Dream*, where provided the modern texts set Q1's 'thorough', the scansion pattern of elegant magic can be established, whereas F1's more plebeian 'through' sets up a much more awkward and clumsy moment.

These texts will set the F1 reading, and footnote where the modern texts' sub-stitution of a different word formation has the potential to alter the meaning (and sometimes scansion) of the line.

'THEN' AND 'THAN'

These two words, though their neutral vowels sound different to modern ears, were almost identical to Elizabethan speakers and readers, despite their different meanings. Ff and Qq make little distinction between them, setting them inter-changeably. In these scripts the original printings will be used, and the modern reader should soon get used to substituting one for the other as necessary.

'I', AND 'AY'

Ff / Qq often print the personal pronoun 'I' and the word of agreement 'aye' sim-ply as 'I'. Again, the modern reader should quickly get used to this and make the sub-stitution whenever necessary. The reader should also be aware that very occasionally either word could be used and the phrase make perfect sense, even though differ-ent meanings would be implied.

'MY SELFE/HIM SELFE/HER SELFE' VERSUS 'MYSELF/HIMSELF/HERSELF'

Generally Ff/Qq separate the two parts of the word, 'my selfe' while most modern texts set the single word 'myself'. The difference is vital, based on Elizabethan philosophy. Elizabethans regarded themselves as composed of two parts, the corporeal 'I', and the more spiritual part, the 'selfe'. Thus when an Elizabethan character refers to 'my selfe', he or she is often referring to what is to all intents and purposes a separate being, even if that being is a particular part of him- or herself. Thus soliloquies can be thought of as a debate between the 'I' and 'my selfe', and in such speeches, even though there may be only one character onstage, it's as if there were two distinct entities present.

These texts will show F1 as set.

FOOTNOTE CODE
(shown in two forms, the first alphabetical, the second grouping the codes by topic)

To help the reader focus on a particular topic or research aspect, a special code has been developed for these texts. Each footnote within the footnote section at the bottom of each page of text has a single letter or series of letters placed in front of it guiding readers to one specific topic; thus 'SPD' will direct readers to footnotes just dealing with songs, poems, and doggerel.

ALPHABETICAL FOOTNOTE CODING

A	asides .
AB	abbreviation
ADD	a passage modern texts have added to their texts from F2–4/Qq
ALT	a passage (including act and scene division) that has been altered by modern texts without any Ff/Qq authority
COMP	a setting probably influenced by compositor interference
F	concerning disputed facts within the play
FL	foreign language
L	letter or letters
LS	alterations in line structure
M	Shakespeare's use of the scansion of magic (trochaic and seven syllables)
N	a name modern texts have changed or corrected for easier recognition
O	F1 words or phrases substituted for a Qq oath or blasphemy
OM	passage, line, or word modern texts omit or suggest omitting
P	change in prefix assigned to a character
PCT	alterations to F1's punctuation by modern and/or contemporary texts
Q	material rejected or markedly altered by Qq not usually set by modern texts
QO	oaths or blasphemies set in Qq not usually set by modern texts
SD	stage directions added or altered by modern texts
SP	a solo split line for a single character (see pp. xv–xvi above)

SPD	matters concerning songs, poems, or doggerel
?ST	where, because of question marks within the passage, the final choice as to the number of sentences is left to the reader's discretion
STRUCT	a deliberate change from the F1 setting by these texts
UE	an unusual entrance (set to the side of the text) or exit (set on a separate line)
VP	F1's verse altered to prose or vice versa, or lines indistinguishable as either
W	F1's word or phrase altered by modern texts
WHO	(in a convoluted passage) who is speaking to whom
WS	F1 line structure altered because of casting off problems (see pp. x–xi above)

FOOTNOTE CODING BY TOPIC

STAGE DIRECTIONS, ETC.

A	asides
P	change in prefix assigned to a character
SD	stage directions added or altered by modern texts
UE	an unusual entrance (set to the side of the text) or exit (set on a separate line)
WHO	(in a convoluted passage) who is speaking to whom

LINE STRUCTURE AND PUNCTUATION, ETC.

L	letter or letters
LS	alterations in line structure
M	Shakespeare's use of the scansion of magic (trochaic and seven syllables)
PCT	alterations to F1's punctuation by modern and/or contemporary texts
SPD	matters concerning songs, poems, or doggerel
?ST	where, because of question marks within the passage, the final choice as to the number of sentences is left to the reader's discretion
SP	a solo split line for a single character (see pp. xv–xvi above)
VP	F1's verse altered to prose or vice versa, or lines indistinguishable as either

| WS | F1 line structure altered because of casting off problems (see pp. x–xi above) |

CHANGES TO WORDS AND PHRASES

AB	abbreviation
F	concerning disputed facts within the play
FL	foreign language
N	a name modern texts have changed or corrected for easier recognition
O	F1 words or phrases substituted for a Qq oath or blasphemy
QO	oaths or blasphemies set in Qq not usually set by modern texts
W	F1's word or phrase altered by modern texts

CHANGES ON A LARGER SCALE AND OTHER UNAUTHORISED CHANGES

ADD	a passage modern texts have added to their texts from F2–4/Qq
ALT	a passage (including act and scene division) that has been altered by modern texts without any Ff/Qq authority
COMP	a setting probably influenced by compositor interference
OM	passage, line, or word modern texts omit or suggest omitting
Q	material rejected or markedly altered by Qq not usually set by modern texts
STRUCT	a deliberate change from the F1 setting by these texts

ONE MODERN CHANGE FREQUENTLY NOTED IN THESE TEXTS

'MINUTE' CHANGES TO THE SYLLABLE LENGTH OF FF LINES

As noted above on pages xi–xii, modern texts frequently correct what commentators consider to be large scale metric deficiencies, often to the detriment of character and scene. There are many smaller changes made too, especially when lines are either longer or shorter than the norm of pentameter by 'only' one or two syllables. These changes are equally troublesome, for there is a highly practical theatrical rule of thumb guideline to such irregularities, viz.:

if lines are slightly **longer** than pentameter, then the characters so involved have too much information coursing through them to be contained within the 'norms' of proper verse, occasionally even to the point of losing self-control

if lines are slightly **shorter** than ten syllables, then either the information therein contained or the surrounding action is creating a momentary (almost need to breath) hesitation, sometimes suggesting a struggle to maintain self-control

These texts will note all such alterations, usually offering the different syllable counts per line as set both by F1 and by the altered modern texts, often with a brief suggestion as to how the original structural 'irregularity' might reflect onstage action.

FINALLY, A BRIEF WORD ABOUT THE COMPOSITORS [9]

Concentrated research into the number of the compositors and their habits began in the 1950s and, for a while, it was thought five men set the First Folio, each assigned a letter, 'A' through 'E'.

'E' was known to be a seventeen-year-old apprentice whose occasional mishaps both in copying text and securing the type to the frame have led to more than a few dreadful lapses, notably in *Romeo and Juliet*, low in the left column on p. 76 of the Tragedies, where in sixteen F1 lines he commits seven purely typographical mistakes. Compositor 'B' set approximately half of F1, and has been accused of being cavalier both with copying text and not setting line ending punctuation when the line is flush to the column edge. He has also been accused of setting most of the so called 'solo' split lines, though a comparison of other compositors' habits suggests they did so too, especially the conglomerate once considered to be the work of a single compositor known as 'A'. It is now acknowledged that the work set by 'A' is probably the work of at least two and more likely five different men, bringing the total number of compositors having worked on F1 to nine ('A' times five, and 'B' through 'E').

It's important to recognise that the work of these men was sometimes flawed. Thus the footnotes in these texts will point the reader to as many examples as possible which current scholarship and research suggest are in error. These errors fall into two basic categories. The first is indisputable, that of pure typographical mistakes ('wh?ch' for 'which'): the second, frequently open to challenge, is failure to copy exactly the text (Qq or manuscript) which F1 has used as its source material.

As for the first, these texts place the symbol † before a footnote marker within the text (not in the footnote section), a combination used only to point to a purely typographical mistake. Thus in the error-riddled section of *Romeo and Juliet* quoted above, p. 109 of this script shows fourteen footnote markers, seven of them coupled with the symbol †. Singling out these typographical-only markers alerts the reader to compositor error, and that (usually) the 'correct' word or phrase has been set within the text. Thus the reader doesn't have to bother with the footnote below unless they have a morbid curiosity to find out what the error actually is. Also, by definition, the more † appearing in a passage, the worse set that passage is.

As to the second series of (sometimes challengeable) errors labelled poor copy work, the footnotes will alert the reader to the alternative Qq word or phrase usage preferred by most modern texts, often discussing the alternatives in detail, especially when there seems to be validity to the F1 setting.

---

[9]   Readers are directed to the ground breaking work of Alice Walker, and also to the ongoing researches of Paul Werstine and Peter W. M. Blayney.

Given the fluid state of current research, more discoveries are bound to be published as to which compositor set which F1 column long after these texts go to print. Thus the current assignation of compositors at the bottom of each of these scripts' pages represents what is known at this moment, and will be open to reassessment as time goes by.

A CAVEAT: THE COMPOSITORS AND 'SINGLE SPLIT LINES' (SEE PP. XV–XVI)

Many commentators suggest single split lines are not Shakespearean dramatic necessity, but compositorial invention to get out of a typesetting dilemma. Their argument is threefold:

first, as mentioned on pp. x–xi, because of 'white space' a small amount of text would have to be artificially expanded to fill a large volume of what would otherwise be empty space: therefore, even though the column width could easily accommodate regular verse lines, the line or lines would be split in two to fill an otherwise embarrassing gap

second, even though the source documents the compositors were using to set F1 showed material as a single line of verse, occasionally there was too much text for the F1 column to contain it as that one single line: hence the line had to be split in two

third, the device was essentially used by compositor B.

There is no doubt that sometimes single split lines did occur for typesetting reasons, but it should be noted that:

single split lines are frequently set well away from white space problems

often the 'too-much-text-for-the-F1-column-width' problem is solved by setting the last one or two words of the overly lengthy line either as a new line, or as an overflow or underflow just above the end of the existing line without resorting to the single split line

all compositors seem to employ the device, especially the conglomerate known as 'A' and compositor F.

As regards the following text, while at times readers will be alerted to the fact that typographical problems could have had an influence on the F1 setting, when single split lines occur their dramatic potential will be discussed, and readers are invited to explore and accept or reject the setting accordingly.

INTRODUCTION TO THE TEXT OF
A MIDSOMMER NIGHTS DREAME[1]
pages 145–162 of the Comedy Section of the First Folio[2]
All Act, Scene, and line numbers will refer to the
Applause text below unless otherwise stated.

Current research places the play between number ten and thirteen in the canon, the probable composition during the winter of 1595–96, though some commentators suggest an earlier date between late 1594 and early 1595. These commentators suggest a first performance date of 1595, while the first recorded performance was New Year's Day, 1604, with the play being retitled for the occasion *A Play Of Robin Goodfellow*. In preparing their editions most modern editors have access to three different Elizabethan scripts:

Quarto 1 (Q1) of 1600, a highly regarded text, probably stemming from Shakespeare's working (foul) papers with many of his personal spelling characteristics in evidence; since the script had not yet come into contact with the Playhouse, its one major drawback is its lack of stage directions, especially exits.

Quarto 2 (Q2), an almost direct copy of Q1, was printed in 1619 by William Jaggard (who printed the First Folio four years later) with the utterly false frontispiece claiming a publication date of 1600 under the name of James Roberts; this text is not highly regarded, for apart from following Q1 in nearly every peculiarity of text setting and prefix, it introduces more than sixty verbal 'errors' when compared to the Q1 text, word changes that cannot be justified by theatrical or authorial rethinking.

First Folio (F1) of 1623: this text has a checkered reputation, for while its usefulness as a speaking text is denied by some (who suggest that not only does it repeat Q2's verbal 'errors', it adds a further fifty of its own), there is no doubt that its thirty extra stage directions, its reassigning of Philostrate's part (see p. xlv below) and even some of its word changes stem from an authority other than that of Q1, an authority which at times has the definite flavour of the Playhouse; the consensus is that whoever prepared this particular play for Folio publication used both Q2 and a Playhouse copy, sometimes

---

[1] For a detailed examination, see Stanley Wells and Gary Taylor, eds., *William Shakespeare: A Textual Companion* (Oxford: Clarendon Press, 1987), 288–305; for a detailed analysis of the play's contents, see any of the Recommended Modern Texts suggested at the end of the Introduction.

[2] *Mr. William Shakespeare's Comedies, Histories, & Tragedies,* 1623.

haphazardly collating both, and probably did not understand theatre too well, hence the (apparently) somewhat peculiar setting of a few of the new stage directions several lines before or after the point at which modern editors assume the action was to take place.

After correcting what can be safely called obvious mistakes, the numerous alterations faced by modern editors can be divided into the two main categories of alternative word choices or minor emendations.

The emendations fall into five basic types: two stem from changes evident when comparing Q1–2 with F1,

word order reversals, 'I do' instead of 'do I'

contractions or expansions, 'he is' to 'he's', and, vice versa, 'he's' to 'he is', while the remainder are 'tidyings' often occasioned by modern editors, and sometimes by the editors of F3 and F4:

the modernising of archaisms, 'do' instead of 'doth'

standardising a plural **verb** to a plural **noun,** 'wits faints' to 'wits faint', and vice versa

altering a verb from past to present, 'seem'd' to 'seem', and vice versa.

About half of F1 was set by compositor C, the remainder equally by B and D. There are occasional minor typographical problems. Thus in a section from the lower right-hand column of p. 160 in the first Folio, compositor C ran out of the lower case letter 'w', and inventively set twenty pairs of double 'v' as a 'vv' instead. Also, compositors D and B each set a page number incorrectly. D lists p. 153 as a second 151, while the first and correctly numbered p. 151 has already been set, containing the end of Act Two and the beginning of Act Three. B lists p. 161 as 163, which in correct numerical order is the first page of *The Merchant of Venice*.

Thus commentators and editors tend to ignore Q2, try to use F1 only when absolutely necessary, especially as regards stage directions, and accept Q1 as the prime substantive text. However, despite its cleanliness and authority, Q1 is a literary text, whereas F1 has obviously been influenced by theatrical considerations and may be used with due caution. To quote from Professor R. A. Foakes' introduction to his *New Cambridge Shakespeare A Midsummer Night's Dream* (see Recommended Texts, below), 'It is a pity that the editor of the Folio text was so casual, though editors have over reacted to what Brooks calls his 'demonstrable negligence and clumsiness'.

The main body of this text will present the material as set in F1. The alternative word choices and the minor emendations will be noted via footnotes within the body of this text. Footnotes will also mark where Q2 offers an interesting reading which could significantly alter the F1 text and which has not been picked up by the modern texts.

It is strongly recommended that the reader not make a silent decision but speak the various alternatives out loud to hear and feel which sits best on the tongue and in the body, for the scripts were created for the purpose of being spoken aloud to a large theatrical audience: what sits well in the head may not have the same impact in the heat of passionate public utterance.

THE NAMING OF NAMES

Modern texts rarely show how and when the prefixes of the characters change in the early texts, and in no other play are characters, whether fairy, regal, mortal, or low-caste working man, so ill-served by the modern editions. For, apart from the four lovers, Qq/Ff are in almost complete agreement as to when and how they give at least two different sets of names (both in prefix and stage direction) to most of the remaining characters. In all cases in this text the Ff prefixes will be given, and a notation made when a prefix change occurs.

THE MECHANICALS

Initially such double naming may seem appropriate, since they all are given parts in the play within the play, but even here there are surprises:

Peter Quince is usually given a prefix that denotes his surname, Quince. However, in the moment he starts coaching Flute as Thisbie, the prefix he is given reflects his first name, Peter, which might just suggest a change in his attitude or behaviour, especially after the more experienced (and officious) Bottome has momentarily left the rehearsal.

Francis Flute is usually given a prefix that denotes his surname, Flute. Naturally, in *Pyramus and Thisbie* he is given his character's prefix denoting Thisbie, yet quite wonderfully this begins to bleed from the rehearsal and play situation into his 'real' life, notably the scene the modern texts call Act Four Scene 2 (this text p. 66). Both the stage direction for his entry into this non-*Pyramus and Thisbie* scene, and the prefixes throughout, refer to him as 'Thisbie'—a clear case of art impinging upon life. Certainly, it offers glorious onstage possibilities for a character (Flute) who is beginning to blur the distinction between the part played, Thisbie, and himself.

Nick Bottome is usually given the prefix denoting his surname, Bottome, or the character he plays, Pyramus. However, at the top of Act Four Scene 1, p. 57, as he enters in the Ass-head, having spent some time with Titania and her entourage, he is titled both in stage direction and prefix as Clowne. This could be a wonderful clue as to how his new airs and graces are seen by reader (and possibly those around him) as he begins to ask all the Fairies to perform favours for him (pp. 57–58), a far cry from his earlier fear in Act Three Scene 1 (pp. 34–36).

THE ARISTOCRATS

The distinctions in prefix for Theseus and Hippolita are equally useful:

Theseus, although occasionally termed Duke in the stage directions, is constantly referred to as Theseus in the prefixes until the moment just before the start of the play within the play (this text p. 73) when the prefix reminds the actor of his rank, indicating Duke. However, rather splendidly, this is immediately forgotten as soon as Quince begins his first dreadful Prologue, the prefix 'Duke' not reappearing until Wall exits (this text p. 77), and this status-enhancing prefix now remains for the rest of the play; perhaps a certain 'noblesse oblige' is thus implied.

The prefix for **Hippolita** remains as Hippolita until Theseus switches for the second time, and then she assumes a regal stature, matching his title with the prefix of Dutchess (p. 78).

THE FAIRIES

It is in this world that the most changes are to be found.

Robin Goodfellow And/Or Pucke

In this tantalising world of prefix alternatives, this is the character best served by Qq/Ff and most damaged by modern texts. There are two sides to him. 'Robin Goodfellow' is one; a contemporary description of him quoted in *An Encyclopedia Of Fairies* describes him in this guise as harmless, possessing powers 'to be used against the ill-disposed . . . in aid of honest folks'.[3] Then there is 'Pucke', described in the same book as a little more malevolent, akin to 'hobgoblins', who although good-natured and predisposed to help people are 'rather nasty people to annoy'.[4] The actor's ability to play both aspects, and to be able to switch back and forth between them, is fundamental to the character's growth throughout the play.

There are nine shifts in his prefix, and occasionally they even change rapidly within one brief piece of stage action. For example, it is Robin who spots the Mechanicals in their rehearsal, but something happens within him to transform him into his alter ego Pucke, who turns Bottome into an ass and consequently destroys the rehearsal. Similarly, it is Pucke who first confronts us, as audience, at the end of the play before the remaining Fairies enter, but it is Robin who asks for the audience's applause and forgiveness in the final epilogue.

His growth is fascinating. He is usually given the prefix of the perhaps less dangerous, less willful, more subservient Robin in dealing with Oberon. But as the play wears on, he begins to stand up for himself as Pucke, notably when attaching equal blame to Oberon for the mess of the two human men (Lysander and Demetrius), both being led to woo Helena through the force of Oberon's magic charm. Also, a wonderful developmental note: though at first it is only as Pucke that the character can perform the magic spells, by the end of the play the gentler Robin can too, admittedly after a very clumsy start, p. 55 this text.

---

[3]   Katharine Briggs, *An Encyclopedia of Fairies* (New York: Pantheon Books, 1976), pp. 341–43.

[4]   Ibid., p. 223.

The modern texts standardise his prefixes to 'Puck'. In those texts these character shifts never appear, and a reader/actor will find it near impossible to discover when and where the distinct personalities might get the upper hand and/or break loose.

To help counterbalance the loss, here is a brief chart of what scene or part of the scene the character is in (by modern scene numbers); what the action is; and what the prefix is that both Q1 and F use. The page number refers to where in this text the prefix can be found.

Scene		Location/Incident	Prefix	Page #
2.1.	a	teasing and bragging with Titania's Fairy	Robin	14
	b	with angry Oberon with the magic herb	Pucke	19
	c	leaving/returning to Oberon with the magic herb	"	22
	d	finding and putting the spell on Lysander	"	26
3.1.	a	first words about the Mechanicals and their play	Robin	32
	b	talking about turning Bottome to a 'stranger Piramus'	Pucke[5]	33
	c	chasing the Mechanicals and Bottome (now the Asse)	"[6]	34
3.3.	a	telling Oberon about Titania, Bottome, and the Mechanicals	Pucke	38
	b	reproaching Oberon for doubting he had 'magicked' the mortals too	Robin	39
	c	realising he has 'magicked' the wrong man	"	41
	d	blamed by Oberon for getting the wrong man and told to get Helena	"	41
	e	bringing her in	Pucke	42
	f	correctly blaming Oberon after all the lovers quarrel	"	51
	g	creating the overcast night spell to bring the lovers together	"	52
	h	teasing the lovers/releasing Lysander from the spell	Robin	53
4.1.		with the reunited Oberon and Titania/releasing Bottome	Robin	59
5.1.	a	first entry to Theseus' palace, with 'broom to clean'	Pucke	84
	b	final farewell to the audience	Robin	85

If ever there was a need for the modern texts to maintain the prefix switches of Qq/Ff it is here. Unfortunately, none of the major texts print the variations, and thus much of Robin/Pucke's development and action is lost.

---

[5] Q1 incorrectly assigns this to Peter Quince.

[6] Q1 sets this as 'Robin', the only time Quarto and Folio disagree as to which of the two inner personalities has the upper hand.

The Remainder of the Fairy World

The speaking/singing parts for **individual Fairies** in Titania's entourage are not always assigned names, especially in the opening of the play with Pucke, p. 14; in the Lullaby, p. 23; and in the first greeting with Bottome, p. 36. The modern texts dutifully assign names and/or numbers, though the original texts allow reader and director to let imagination roam free.

Oberon is only described by the prefix of his given name, Oberon. Occasionally he is addressed by his title King of the Fairies, which is also used in a few stage directions, and the reasons for so doing are usually very apparent in the text.

Titania is referred to only by the (rather daunting) title Queene until she awakes under the influence of the love spell that Oberon has placed upon her. From then on the prefix only reflects her name, Titania, and never her title or rank even when she is released from the drug-induced love and returns to her (presumably) true and natural love, Oberon. The two prefixes seem to have enormous implications for the playing of the role, especially at the start of the play.

THE LANGUAGE OF MAGIC

Whenever magic is used in the plays (notably in *The Tempest* and *Macbeth* in addition to this play) the form of the spoken verse markedly changes. The normal pattern is akin to five pairs of human heartbeats (technically, the ten syllables of a regular Shakespeare verse line are known as iambic pentameter, with the ten syllables being arranged in five pairs of beats, each pair alternating a pattern of a weak stress followed by a strong stress). When magic is used the line alters in two ways:

the length is usually reduced from ten to just seven syllables, and

the pattern of stresses is completely reversed, as if the heartbeat was being forced either by the circumstances of the scene or by the need of the speaker to completely change direction.

Thus the emphasis as Oberon begins to enchant Titania would be on the capitalised words 'WHAT thou SEEST when THOU dost WAKE', p. 24, l. 2.1.308.

There are several fascinating aspects to the language of magic in this play:

When the fairy characters make the move from regular speech to the patterns of spoken magic, it is usually apparent why. But **how easy** is it for them to do so, especially the 'junior' fairies such as Pucke and the members of Titania's entourage? Also, what physical and mental state does the magic create in them as they both start and finish?

The magic cannot always be sustained, especially by Robin/Pucke, and when breaks occur it is very useful to ask what is happening theatrically to cause such a break.

The magic does not always occur when the audience expects it, for example the Fairies' song on p. 23, and perhaps the Fairie that Pucke meets (footnote #1 p. 16).

Not everyone can use it whenever they wish: Titania's first magical utterance does not occur until after she is released from Oberon's spell (p. 61, starting l. 4.1.113 of this script). For her to be unable to utilise magic until so late in the play lends all the more force to her first major speech, dealing with how Oberon has disrupted the dances of harmony so necessary for herself and her entourage (ll. 2.1.83–120, pp. 17–18). It also has enormous implications for her own abilities and powers within the play up to this moment. And it marks the wonderful release which leads her (and not Oberon as sometimes set by modern texts) to speak and teach all the Fairies from both entourages the final magical song of blessing.

To help the reader recognise the patterns of 'magical' speech this script will bold and footnote the text whenever they occur.

PHILOSTRATE OR EGEUS?

Q1 shows two distinct characters: Egeus the father of Hermia; and Philostrate, a court official, the manager of entertainments to divert Theseus. By the time of the First Folio, although Philostrate is still addressed by name in the first scene (p. 1, l. 12), his speaking part has been reduced to just one speech (p. 72, ll. 5.1.92–97). His other lines have been redistributed in two ways: to Egeus, and to whoever reads the list of entertainments to pass away the first part of the marriage night (footnote #1, p. 71).

It is safe to assume that the additional text used in preparing F1 had a speaking part removed because of company size and/or economy, but the problem still remains, whether to maintain both characters (as in Q1) or to reassign everything including the single F1 Philostrate speech. Some modern texts follow Q1; others follow F1 and assign Philostrate's remaining Act Five speech to Egeus.

THE PLAY WITHIN THE PLAY, AND WHAT EXACTLY IS 'EIGHT AND SIXE'

PRESENTATION IN THIS TEXT

Neither Qq nor Ff make any typeface distinction for the setting of the Mechanicals play within the play, *Piramus and Thisbie*. Occasionally, especially in the so-called rehearsal sequence, Act Three Scene 1, pp. 33–34, at first glance it is not always clear whether the dialogue is *A Midsommer Nights Dreame* or *Pyramus and Thisbie*. Thus, for the purposes of clarity, this text will set the Mechanicals play in **a**

---

[7]   Op. cit., p. xxviii, footnotes #2, #3, #4.

[8]   Op. cit., p. 651.

slightly smaller type than the rest of the text. In addition, **both the roles and names of the actors' playing them will be set, and slightly further indented,** to distinguish them from those shown for the other characters watching either the rehearsal or performance.

EIGHT AND SIXE

Pyramus and Thisbie is written in two different rhythmic styles. A reasonably close approximation of ten-syllable iambic pentameter lines opens the piece. However, towards the end, as both Pyramus and Thisbie bewail their fates and commit suicide, their purple passages (the content of which is bad/funny enough in and of itself) are set in what most modern texts show as two four-syllable rhyming lines, followed by a third line of six syllables. The rhyme of this third line is then matched in two more lines time.

Thus as Pyramus/Bottome begins his perorations, most modern texts set

But stay: O spight!	(4)
But marke, poore Knight,	(4)
What dreadful dole is heere?	(6)
Eyes do you see?	(4)
How can it be!	(4)
O dainty Ducke: O Deere!	(6)

(p. 80, ll. 5.1.306–10)

a form of very bad doggerel. This, when played to the hilt, raises a lot of laughter at, rather than with, the performers, when it should be at the content. Yet both Duke and Dutchess, who hitherto were making rude comments about the piece, say publicly how affected they are:

Duke	This passion, and the death of a deare friend,
	Would go neere to make a man looke sad.
Dutchess	Beshrew my heart, but I pittie the man.

(p. 81, ll. 5.1.315–17)

Given their earlier reactions, and the normal result of playing the doggerel set in most modern texts, it is going to be difficult for them not to appear as hypocrites, unless something in the playing style really does affect them.

Earlier, Peter Quince is badgered by Bottome for extra lines, Act Three Scene 1, p. 30. If Bottome cannot play all the parts as he offered earlier in the casting meeting (Act One Scene 2, pp. 10–11) at least this time he gets his wish in the form of a Prologue, which Quince promises to write in 'eight and sixe', l. 3.1.24. This promise seems to have slipped past most commentators, and many theatre people regard this as a (broken) promise to write Bottome a sonnet in the Italianate style, eight lines in the first idea and six in the second.

But in fact Quince does write in 'eight and sixe', not as a sonnet, but as an archaic form of metric scansion, the splendidly dreadful purple passage finales for Bottome/Pyramus and Flute/Thisbie. Thus, in this archaic form, the opening to Bottome's speech would now read as:

But stay: O spight! But marke, poore Knight,	(8)
What dreadful dole is heere?	(6)
Eyes do you see? How can it be!	(8)
O dainty Ducke: O Deere!	(6)

and all of a sudden the still dreadful content is now wrapped in a more noble poetic form, which would occasion the response that it does from Theseus and Hippolita (as Duke and Dutchess), and direct the laughter more with the characters and at the material.

And this 'eight and sixe' verse is exactly how Qq/Ff set the speeches. Needless to say, this text will set Qq/Ff as is, mark the modern alterations, and allow the readers to make their own choice.

FACTUAL NIGGLES

None of these have shattering implications, yet, as with the minor metrical and rhetorical alterations shown below, their cumulative effect can have a great impact on character and play, as the first example clearly shows.

A problem lies in assigning who actually reads **the list of dreadful entertainments** offered the three newly married couples to while away the evening before, at last, going to bed. Though the moment is relatively minor, the choices are varied, ranging from the pomposity of a Philostrate, the disbelief of a Theseus, a tongue-in-cheek Lysander, or a sharing of the abominations by all. The alternatives are offered in footnote #1 p. 71.

Qq/Ff texts give no clear indication as to who sings what in the songs (see footnotes #4, p. 23 and #2, p. 85). Indeed, what Qq/Ff seem to set as the final song, p. 85, most modern texts regard as a separate speech.

Though at their first appearance Oberon (in addition to Pucke) and Titania (in addition to the Fairie) are assigned 'traines' to accompany them (p. 16), the number of fairies are not specified. Four are named later with Titania, but an F1 misreading of a Q1 stage direction adds a further four to her entourage. Most modern texts accept Q1's reading, and restrict her attendants to four (see footnote #1, p. 36).

Two other **stage directions** also create minor problems. The first, as to whether the twice repeated 'Stand Forth' on p. 2 is dialogue or stage direction is a matter of reader choice (see footnote #1 p. 2). The second concerns what apparently is the double entry of Pucke and Robin into the rehearsal of *Pyramus and Thisbie,* and when and how he brings the newly transformed Bottome onto the stage: see the discussion under Pucke above, pp. xlii–xliii, and also footnotes #5, p. 31; #2, p. 32; and #1 and #6, p. 34.

STANDARD MODERN TEXT TIDYING OF THE FIRST FOLIO

Modern alterations to this text in spelling standardisation, line structure, punctuation, and verse and prose are tiny, but their cumulative effect can alter tremendously the small details that add colour and variety to the action. For all the following examples, this text will set F1 throughout, and footnote the changes accordingly.

WORDS

Choice

There is a lovely reading from Q1 not accepted by either F1 or most modern texts, which may go a long way to explain what has long been a critical quagmire: why Demetrius remains in love with the once-deserted Helena after he has been 'de-magic-ed'. F1 and all modern texts set as one of his early 'pre-magic' rejection lines to her

>   doe I not in plainest truth
>   Tell you I doe not, nor I cannot love you.
>
>   (p. 21, ll. 209–10)

which seems a fairly heartfelt rebuttal. Q1 sets one word differently, changing F1's final 'nor' to 'not', and the whole line and their potential relationship has a totally different possibility:

>   doe I not in plainest truth
>   Tell you I doe not, not I cannot love you.

Variable Spellings

With three compositors, it is foolish to suggest every spelling difference has significance. Yet, when one compositor sets the same word in three different ways, the moment is well worth exploring, especially when Bottome in his prefix as Clowne is involved. First transformed into an Asse, then having been led as a lover to Titania's Bower, and now described as Clowne, Bottome is requesting various favours from the Fairies of whom he was originally afraid. Addressing them all by the French honorific which most modern texts spell as 'Monsieur', F1's compositor C shows Bottome speaking the variations 'Mounsiueur', 'Mounsier', and 'Mounsieur' (ll. 4.1.8–20, p. 57).

Readers may decide whether the variations are 'accidentals' caused by spacing problems within First Folio left-hand column on p. 157, which doesn't seem to be a factor in this case; or in fact an invitation to play with sounds — especially if Bottome is sleepy, as indeed he says he is by l. 4.1.49.

Much more care should be taken when examining the spellings of characters' names. Doublets abound. Thus the following can clearly be established throughout the play for the human and fairy characters:

The shorter **Titania** is the normal form when others speak her name; the longer Tytania is much less used (though this spelling is used as a prefix).

The shorter **Snout** is the normal form; Snowt is the longer, less used, spelling by which he describes himself, a form of self-aggrandisement, perhaps.

The shorter **Snug** is the normal form; Snugge is the longer, less used, spelling.

The longer **Pucke** is the normal form; the shorter Puck is the less used spelling.

The longer **Bottome** is the normal form; the shorter Bottom is the less used spelling.

While in the play within the play,

the shorter **Piramus** is the normal form; the longer Pyramus the less used spelling.

Readers are warned that most commentators loathe the idea of variables in spelling being used as guides to pronunciation. Unless the variations are set on the same column by the same compositor, differences should be approached very cautiously. However, when the same compositor is involved, as above with compositor C, then explorations might be safely made,[7] viz.:

the character played by Flute is referred to almost equally in the foreshortened form of **Thisbie** or **Thisbe** (a hushed reverence perhaps) and the slightly longer (more everyday?) **Thisby:** in the right-hand column of p. 147 of the First Folio, p. 11 this text, there are two different spellings of the same name as the parts are handed out: very occasionally there is the much longer reference to Thysby.

Elizabethan Word Substitutions

Finally, on p. xxxi of the General Introduction a list is shown of alternative words. Several have an impact on this play, including 'through' and 'thorough', which could affect so-called magical lines on p. 14; 'spirit' and 'sprite', which could affect the rhythm of certain lines throughout; and 'ballet' and 'ballad', which has a decisive influence on whether Bottome wishes to sing or dance for the Duke at the wedding day festivities.

MISSING AND REVERSED LINE ORDERS

One guaranteed laugh line set by Q1 is omitted by Ff. At the end of the lovers' quarrel, the two women are left alone, and F1 gives Helena the last word, and laugh, with her cat-fight avoiding exit:

---

[7]   See Neil Freeman, *Shakespeare's First Texts* (Vancouver: Folio Scripts, 1994), available from Applause Books.

> Your hands then mine, are quicker for a fray,
> My legs are longer though to runne away.
> (p. 50, ll. 3.1. 602–3)

Doubly rejected by the men, and now rejected by her onetime friend, Q1 allows Hermia a final bedraggled thought before leaving the stage:

> I am amaz'd, and know not what to say.

Most modern texts rightfully include the missing line.

However, their changes in line order leave something to be desired. Here is Lysander persuading Hermia to run away with him. Qq/Ff set the following:

> I have a Widdow Aunt, a dowager,
> Of great revennew, and she hath no childe,
> From Athens is her house remov'd seven leagues,
> And she respects me, as her onely sonne:
> (p. 6, ll. 1.1.162–65)

Modern texts reverse the last two lines

> And she respects me, as her onely sonne:
> From Athens is her house remov'd seven leagues,

thus putting possibly unwarranted logic in what the first texts suggest is a case of the mind jumping forwards and backwards as the ideas hit.

However, it does take a bigger leap of faith to stay with F1/Q2's version of the just awoken, newly 'magic-ed' Titania as she praises the beauty of (Bottome as) the Asse's singing (!) and appearance (!!), pp. 35–36, ll. 3.1.153–57. Here most modern texts prefer Q1's logical order of

> I pray thee gentle mortall, sing againe,
> Mine eare is much enamored of thy note;
> So is mine eye enthralled to thy shape.
> And thy fair vertues force (perforce) doth move me
> On the first view to say, to sweare I love thee.

rather than the all over the place craziness of Q2/Ff

> I pray thee gentle mortall, sing againe,
> Mine eare is much enamored of thy note;
> On the first view to say, to sweare I love thee.
> So is mine eye enthralled to thy shape.
> And thy fair vertues force (perforce) doth move me.

In all such cases, F1 will be set as is, and the modern alterations will be footnoted and discussed.

VERSE AND PROSE

The world of verse, with its attempts at grace and dignity, and that of prose, the more realistic, prosaic practical side of life, are usually clearly separated in this play. It's no accident that the Mechanicals only speak verse when they attempt to perform their play, and if they fall out of the text, as does Starveling as Mooneshine, they revert to prose, with one notable exception as exampled below. It's no accident that the fairies never speak anything other than verse, nor that the humans fall into prose as they make their rather rude remarks about the Mechanicals play. So, whenever there are (the few) Qq/Ff transgressions, they are well worth exploring

The clearest separation between the two comes in the final intertwined moments of the still-enchanted Titania and the spell-bound Bottome as Asse. She offers him the delicacies of the Fairy world; he wants the grosser earthly delights that usually result in breaking wind (p. 58, ll. 4.1.43–49). Her offer is in irregular verse, his reply is in earth-bound prose—at least in Ff. Q1 shows her speaking prose too (though both this and her following speech are crammed together at the bottom of the Q page, suggesting space problems). Some modern texts accept neither F1 nor Q1 and set both characters in verse. Thus readers have three choices, the Ff setting seeming to mark the most difference between the characters.

There is also a wonderful moment in the play *Pyramus and Thisbie* as Flute seems to miss his cue to enter. Replying to Thescus' suggestion as to what should happen next, Bottome is emboldened to speak directly to him, p. 76, ll. 210–17.

Qq/Ff offer something quite delightful. Bottom is shown as capable of rising to the moment and perhaps saving the show. Rather than just apologising as himself, as most productions have him do, he stays in character with the prefix of Pyramus, and, for the only time when not in the world of the play within the play, he speaks in verse. A lovely moment if the reader so wishes—a case of art transcending the normal social boundaries, when a play-acted prince (Pyramus) can speak as an equal to a real life ruler (Theseus).

Most modern texts assign him the speech as 'Bottom', and set it as prose.

ALTERATIONS TO THE LINE STRUCTURE

Again, these alterations are infrequent, but highly telling, with modern texts creating regularity when Qq/Ff suggest anything but is taking place. Two cases from the small passage where Hermia has to deal with Demetrius, who is now even more besotted with her (via Pucke's misplaced magic) and wooing her even more ardently, even though he knows she loves Lysander. Qq/Ff reek of melodrama as she suggests (with the line syllable count in brackets)

> If thou hast slaine Lysander in his sleepe, (10)
> Being ore shooes in bloud, plunge in the deepe, and kill me too. (14)
> (p. 39, ll. 3.1.269–71)

which modern texts normalise as

> If thou hast slaine Lysander in his sleepe,   (10)
> Being ore shooes in bloud, plunge in the deepe,   (10)
> And kill me too.   (4)

setting regular pentameter and a pause where overly-long passion first was shown by Qq/Ff.

Qq/Ff's also give her a triumphant exit:

Hermia	I pray thee tell me then that he is well.
Demetrius	And if I could, what should I get therefore?
Hermia	A priviledge, never to see me more;
	And from thy hated presence part I: see me no more (13)
	Whether he be dead or no. (7)

> (p. 41, ll. 3.1.303–7)

where the long line betrays her passion (in fact many directors have her slap his face before leaving) and the short line allows a deathly hush before Demetrius dare open his mouth again. Most modern texts add the word 'so' to create a couplet and set a more regulated finale:

> And from thy hated presence part I so: (11)
> See me no more whether he be dead or no.   (10)

which almost completely undoes the histrionics Ff/Qq allow her.

For an extended passage of very strange irregularity, readers are guided to Theseus' opening speech of Act Five, pp. 69–70. Q1/Ff show him struggling to express himself over matters he has never voiced before; most modern texts smooth his excitement almost completely away.

SPLIT LINES SET FOR A SINGLE CHARACTER

As discussed on pp. xv–xvi of the General Introduction, this basically Ff device has great potential in highlighting a moment of thought or action for a single character. Two quick examples here will suffice, surrounding the first meeting of the ever-quarrelsome Oberon and Titania. In reply to Pucke's 'But roome Fairy, heere comes Oberon', most modern texts set the last comment from Titania's Fairie and Oberon's first, not especially courteous, greeting as

Fairie	And here my Mistris: Would that he were gone.
Oberon	Ill met by Moone-light, Proud Tytania.

which Ff show as two pairs of split lines:

Fairie	And here my Mistris:
	Would that he were gone.

| Oberon | Ill met by Moone-light, |
| | Proud Tytania. |

(p. 16, ll. 2.1.57–60)

The Ff setting allows the second part of the Fairie's line to be delivered to the audience, after hesitating to ensure no one else overhears, and for Oberon to wait after his first line until he sees what impact his opening bluntness has on both groups of Fairies, his and hers, before continuing.

LINES OF VERSE SHARED BY TWO CHARACTERS

The so-called 'split-line' is not used very often in this play; when it is, for example in the later interchanges between the Lovers in what modern texts refer to as Act Three Scene Two (pp. 47–49 this text), they should be explored to the fullest for their quick response potential (for further details see pp. xii–xv in the General Introduction).

ALTERATIONS TO PUNCTUATION

What is fascinating about this play is that all commentators and editors have recognised the theatrical value of the apparently deliberate setting in the first man-uscripts of the truly abominable and ungrammatical punctuation of Quince's open-ing speech as Prologue, pp. 73–74, ll. 5.1.126–38. As Theseus and Lysander publicly acknowledge, Quince has made a mess of it.

The modern texts recognise the bad phrasing shown by the Qq/Ff punctuation as an essential indication of Quince's nerve-wracked mistakes. The bad punctuation has a dramatic purpose. Indeed, it allows for two things: the appalling irregularity of this section to be played theatrically to the full, and a wonderful contrast when Quince comes back triumphantly, virtually mistake-proof, in his very next speech, pp. 74–5, ll. 5.1.150–77.

Yet other Ff or Ff/Qq 'mistakes' in punctuation are not kept as potentially equally important clues. Through their lack of major punctuation, Qq/Ff show Pucke as all over the place as he recounts to Oberon how he transformed Bottome, and that, even better, it was this creature that the spell-bound Titania fell in love with (pp. 38–9, ll. 3.1.227–56). And an admittedly F1-only peculiarity may add great dignity to a diffi-cult situation that threatens to get out of hand with Hermia's bold contradiction of Theseus as her judge. In the following, the firmness of the two strange (asterisked) periods in Theseus' warning to Hermia as to where her duty lies could save a world of further explanations, and her life:

Theseus	Demetrius is a worthy Gentleman.
Hermia	So is Lysander.
Theseus	In himselfe he is. *
	But in this kinde, wanting your fathers voyce. *
	The other must be held the worthier.

The heavy punctuation after each line suggests Theseus is placing much more emphasis on each short statement than normal (losing his patience perhaps? or even going so far as to carefully spell out to Hermia the legal situation in which she is trapped). No modern text sets the passage as shown.

ACT, SCENE, AND LINE DIVISION

The First Folio provides Act division only, with no further breakdown into Scenes.

Neil Freeman
Vancouver, B. C.
Canada, 1996

RECOMMENDED MODERN TEXTS WITH EXCELLENT SCHOLARLY FOOTNOTES AND RESEARCH

The footnotes in this text are concise, and concentrate either on matters theatrical or choices in word or line structure which distinguish most modern editions and this Folio based text. Items of literary, historical, and linguistic concern have been well researched and are readily available elsewhere. One of the best **research** works in recent years is

Wells, Stanley, and Gary Taylor, eds. *William Shakespeare: A Textual Companion*. Oxford: Clarendon Press, 1987.

In terms of modern **texts,** readers are urged to consult at least one of the following:

Brooks, Harold F., ed. *A Midsummer Night's Dream — The Arden Shakespeare*. London: Methuen & Co. Ltd., 1983.

Evans, Gwynne Blakemore, Harry Levin, Anne Barton, Herschel Baker, Frank Kermode, Hallet D. Smith, and Marie Edel, eds. *The Riverside Shakespeare*. Copyright © 1974 by Houghton Mifflin Company.

Foakes, R. A., ed. *A Midsummer Night's Dream — The New Cambridge Shakespeare*. Cambridge: Cambridge University Press, 1984.

Wells, S. and G. Taylor, eds. *William Shakespeare, The Complete Works*. Oxford: Clarendon Press, Old Spelling Edition 1986; Modern Spelling Edition 1986.

A MIDSOMMER NIGHTS DREAME

Dramatis Personæ

THESEUS, Duke of Athens
HIPPOLITA, Queen of the Amazons, betrothed to Theseus

PHILOSTRATE, an Official in charge of Court Revels

HERMIA, daughter of Egeus, in love with Lysander
LYSANDER, loved by, and in love with Hermia
DEMETRIUS, loved by Helena but now in love with and suitor to Hermia
HELENA, in love with Demetrius

EGEUS, father of Hermia, and supporter of Demetrius

OBERON, King of the Fairies
ROBIN Goodfellow, also known as PUCKE

TITANIA, Queene of the Fairies
PEASE-BLOSSOME ⎫
COBWEB   ⎬ Fairies to Titania
MOTH   ⎪
MUSTARD-SEEDE ⎭

THE MECHANICALS, who play in 'Piramus and Thisbie'

Peter QUINCE, a Carpenter	Prologue
Nick BOTTOME, a Weaver	Piramus
Francis FLUTE, a Bellows Mender	Thisbie
Tom SNOUT, a Tinker	Wall
SNUG, a Joyner	Lyon
Robin STARVELING, a Taylor	Moone-shine

Attendants, Lords, Fairies

mentioned, though given no stage directions to enter are
A Changeling Boy, Huntsmen, and a Forrester

This Cast List has been specially prepared for this edition, and will not be found in any Folio text

A
MIDSOMMER
Nights Dreame

Actus primus

ENTER THESEUS, HIPPOLITA, WITH OTHERS [1]

Theseus

Now[†] faire Hippolita, our nuptiall houre
Drawes on apace: foure happy daies bring in
Another Moon: but oh, me thinkes, how slow
This old Moon wanes; She lingers my desires
Like to a Step-dame, or a Dowager,
Long withering out a yong mans revennew.

Hippolita

Foure daies wil quickly steep théselves[2] in nights[3]
Foure nights wil quickly dreame away the time:
And then the Moone, like to a silver bow,
Now[4] bent in heaven, shal behold the night
Of our solemnities.

Theseus

Go Philostrate,
Stirre up the Athenian youth to merriments,
Awake the pert and nimble spirit of mirth,
Turne melancholy forth to Funerals: [5]
The pale companion is not for our pompe,
Hippolita, I woo'd thee with my sword,
And wonne thy love, doing thee injuries:
But I will wed thee in another key,
With pompe, with triumph, and with revelling.

5

10

15

20

[P 1] since in two speeches time Philostrate is given an order, most modern texts include him in the entry (however see the section 'Philostrate or Egeus' in the Specific Introduction to this play)

[AB 2] F1 = 'théselves', F3/Qq and most modern texts = 'themselves'

[W 3] F1/Q2 = 'nights', Q1 and most modern texts = 'night'

[W 4] F1/Qq = 'Now', most modern texts = 'New'

[SD 5] most modern texts suggest this is where Philostrate leaves

**ENTER EGEUS AND HIS DAUGHTER HERMIA, LYSANDER,
AND DEMETRIUS**

Egeus	Happy be Theseus, our renowned Duke.
Theseus	Thanks good Egeus: what's the news with thee?
Egeus	Full of vexation, come I, with complaint
	Against my childe, my daughter Hermia.

STAND FORTH DEMETRIUS [1]

25 My Noble Lord,
This man hath my consent to marrie her.

STAND FORTH LYSANDER

And my gracious Duke,
This man [2] hath bewitch'd the bosome of my childe:
Thou, thou Lysander, thou hast given her rimes,
30 And interchang'd love-tokens with my childe:
Thou hast by Moone-light at her window sung,
With faining voice, verses of faining love,
And stolne the impression of her fantasie,
With bracelets of thy haire, rings, gawdes, conceits,
35 Knackes, trifles, Nose-gaies, sweet meats (messengers
Of strong prevailment in unhardned youth)   L 145 - b
With cunning hast thou filch'd my daughters heart,
Turn'd her obedience (which is due to me)
To stubborne harshnesse.
40   And my gracious Duke,
Be it so she will not heere before your Grace,
Consent to marrie with Demetrius,
I beg the ancient priviledge of Athens;
As she is mine, I may dispose of her;
45 Which shall be either to this Gentleman,
Or to her death, according to our Law,
Immediately provided in that case.

Theseus	What say you Hermia? be advis'd faire Maide,
	To you your Father should be as a God;
50 | | One that compos'd your beauties; yea and one |

L 145 - b / R 145 - b : 1.1.20 - 48

ALT [1]
  the source texts print this as a stage direction, many modern texts print this (and the exact same direction
  for Lysander two lines later) as a spoken command from Egeus

W [2]
  some modern texts follow F2 and omit the word 'man', thus reducing the line to ten syllables

To whom you are but as a forme in waxe
By him imprinted : and within his power,
To leave the figure, or disfigure it :
Demetrius is a worthy Gentleman .

Hermia   So is Lysander.

Theseus   In himselfe he is.

But in this kinde; wanting your fathers voyce.

The other must be held the worthier. [1]

Hermia   I would my father look'd but with my eyes .

Theseus   Rather your eies must with his judgment looke .

Hermia   I do entreat your Grace to pardon me .

I know not by what power I am made bold,
Nor how it may concerne my modestie
In such a presence heere to pleade my thoughts :
But I beseech your Grace, that I may know
The worst that may befall me in this case,
If I refuse to wed Demetrius .

Theseus   Either to dye the death, or to abjure
For ever the society of men .

Therefore faire Hermia question your desires,
Know of your youth, examine well your blood,
Whether (if you yeeld not to your fathers choice)
You can endure the liverie of a Nunne,
For aye to be in shady Cloister mew'd,
To live a barren sister all your life,
Chanting faint hymnes to the cold fruitlesse Moone,
Thrice blessed they that master so their blood,
To undergo such maiden pilgrimage,
But earthlier happie is the Rose distil'd,
Then that which withering on the virgin thorne,
Growes, lives, and dies, in single blessednesse.   R 145 - b

Hermia   So will I grow, so live, so die my Lord,
Ere I will yeeld my virgin Patent up
Unto his Lordship, whose unwished yoake,
My soule consents not to give soveraignty.

R 145 - b / L 146 - b : 1.1.49 - 82

PCT [1]
F1 is alone in setting a period to end each of the three lines of the speech (perhaps as if Theseus were taking great care to point out each step of the case against Hermia): F2 sets period, nothing, and period: Q/most modern texts set period, comma, period

3

Theseus	Take time to pause, and by the next new Moon
	The sealing day betwixt my love and me,
	For everlasting bond of fellowship:
	Upon that day either prepare to dye,
90	For disobedience to your fathers will,
	Or else to wed Demetrius as hee would,
	Or on Dianaes Altar to protest
	For aie, austerity, and single life.
Demetrius	Relent sweet Hermia, and Lysander, yeelde
95	Thy crazed title to my certaine right.
Lysander	You have her fathers love, Demetrius:
	Let me have Hermiaes: do you marry him.
Egeus	Scornfull Lysander, true, he hath my Love;
	And what is mine, my love shall render him.
100	And she is mine, and all my right of her,
	I do estate unto Demetrius.
Lysander	I am my Lord, as well deriv'd as he,
	As well possest: my love is more then his:
	My fortunes every way as fairely ranck'd
105	(If not with vantage) as Demetrius:
	And (which is more then all these boasts can be)
	I am belov'd of beauteous Hermia.
	Why should not I then prosecute my right?
	Demetrius, Ile avouch it to his head,
110	Made love to Nedars daughter, Helena,
	And won her soule: and she (sweet Ladie) dotes,
	Devoutly dotes, dotes in Idolatry,
	Upon this spotted and inconstant man.
Theseus	I must confesse, that I have heard so much,
115	And with Demetrius thought to have spoke thereof:
	But being over-full of selfe-affaires,
	My minde did lose it.
	But Demetrius come,
	And come Egeus, you shall go with me,
120	I have some private schooling for you both.
	For you faire Hermia, looke you arme your selfe,
	To fit your fancies to your Fathers will;
	Or else the Law of Athens yeelds you up
	(Which by no meanes we may extenuate)
125	To death, or to a vow of single life.

Come my Hippolita, what cheare my love?

Demetrius and Egeus go along:
I must imploy you in some businesse
Against our nuptiall, and conferre with you
30   Of something, neerely that concernes your selves.

Egeus   With dutie and desire we follow you.

[Exeunt]
MANET LYSANDER AND HERMIA

Lysander   How now my love?
                   Why is your cheek so pale?
How chance the Roses there do fade so fast?

35   **Hermia**   Belike for want of raine, which I could well
Beteeme them, from the tempest of mine[1] eyes.

Lysander   For ought that ever I could reade,[2]
Could ever heare by tale or historie,
The course of true love never did run smooth,
140   But either it was different in blood.

Hermia   O crosse! too high to be enthral'd to love.[3]

Lysander   Or else misgraffed, in respect of yeares.

Hermia   O spight! too old to be ingag'd to yong.

Lysander   Or else it stood upon the choise of merit.[4]

145   **Hermia**   O hell! to choose love by anothers eie.[5]

Lysander   Or if there were a simpathie in choise,
Warre, death, or sicknesse, did lay siege to it;
Making it momentarie,[6] as a sound: L 146-b
Swift as a shadow, short as any dreame,
150   Briefe as the lightning in the collied night,

L 146 - b / R 146 - b : 1.1.122 - 145

[1] F1 = 'mine', Qq and most modern texts = 'my'

[2] Qq and most modern texts = ' me: for ought that I could ever reade' ('Eigh' = 'Ay'): F1 = 'For ought that ever I could reade', (reducing the line to 8 syllables)

[3] F1/Qq = 'love', some modern texts = 'low'

[4] F1 = 'merit', Qq and most modern texts = 'friends' (one modern gloss changes the second word 'else' to the F1 word 'merit', viz. 'Or merit stood upon the choice of friends.'

[5] F1 = 'eie', Qq and most modern texts = 'eyes'

[6] F1 = 'momentarie', Qq and most modern texts = 'momentanie'

That (in a spleene) unfolds both heaven and earth;
And ere a man hath power to say, behold,
The jawes of darknesse do devoure it up:
So quicke bright things come to confusion.

Hermia 55

If then true Lovers have beene ever crost,
It stands as an edict in destinie:
Then let us teach our triall patience,
Because it is a customarie crosse,
As due to love, as thoughts, and dreames, and sighes,
60 Wishes and teares; poore Fancies followers.

Lysander

A good perswasion; therefore heare me Hermia,
I have a Widdow Aunt, a dowager,
Of great revennew, and she hath no childe,
From Athens is her house remov'd [1] seven leagues,
65 And she respects me, as her onely sonne: [2]
There gentle Hermia, may I marrie thee,
And to that place, the sharpe Athenian Law
Cannot pursue us.
                  If thou lov'st me, then
70 Steale forth thy fathers house to morrow night:
And in the wood, a league without the towne,
(Where I did meete thee once with Helena,
To do observance for [3] a morne of May)
There will I stay for thee.

Hermia 175

My good Lysander,
I sweare to thee, by Cupids strongest bow,
By his best arrow with the golden head,
By the simplicitie of Venus Doves,
By that which knitteth soules, and prospers love, [4]
180 And by that fire which burn'd the Carthage Queene,
When the false Troyan under saile was seene,
By all the vowes that ever men have broke,
(In number more then ever women spoke)
In that same place thou hast appointed me,
185 To morrow truly will I meete with thee.

Lysander

Keepe promise love: looke here comes Helena.

R 146 - b : 1.1.146 - 179

W [1]
F1 = 'remov'd', Qq and most modern texts = 'remote'

ALT [2]
some modern editions reverse the F1/Qq order of these two lines: the source text shows Lysander
skittering between two topics, the modern texts turn his scattiness into a logical progression

W [3]
F1 = 'for', Qq and most modern texts = 'to'

W [4]
F1/Q2 = 'love', Q1 and most modern texts = 'loves'

6

ENTER HELENA

Hermia	God speede faire Helena, whither away?
Helena	Cal you me faire? that faire againe unsay,
	Demetrius loves you faire:[1] O happie faire!
	Your eyes are loadstarres, and your tongues sweet ayre
	More tuneable then Larke to shepheards eare,
	When wheate is greene, when hauthorne buds appeare,
	Sicknesse is catching: O were favor so,
	Your words I catch,[2] faire Hermia ere I go,
	My eare should catch your voice, my eye, your eye,
	My tongue should catch your tongues sweet melodie,
	Were the world mine, Demetrius being bated,
	The rest Ile[3] give to be to you translated.
	O teach me how you looke, and with what art
	you[4] sway the motion of Demetrius hart.
Hermia	I frowne upon him, yet he loves me still.
Helena	O that your frownes would teach my smiles
	such skil.
Hermia	I give him curses, yet he gives me love.
Helena	O that my prayers could such affection moove.
Hermia	The more I hate, the more he followes me.
Helena	The more I love, the more he hateth me.
Hermia	His folly Helena is none[5] of mine.
Helena	None but your beauty, wold that fault wer mine[6]
Hermia	Take comfort: he no more shall see my face,
	Lysander and myselfe will flie this place.

R 146 - b : 1.1.180 - 203

[W 1] Ff = 'you faire', Q2/most modern texts = 'your faire'

[W 2] F1/Qq = 'Your words I', F2 = 'Your words Ide', most modern texts = 'Yours would I'

[W 3] F1/Qq = 'Ile', most modern texts = 'I'd'

[V P 4] F1's printing of the lower case 'you' (as if it were prose) is not matched by any previous Q text: F2/most modern texts print 'You' - a normal start to a line of verse

[W 5] F1/Q2 = 'none', Q1 and most modern texts = 'no fault' (in addition, some of these modern texts reduce 'Helena' to 'Helen' to maintain the line as ten syllables)

[PCT 6] F1 shows no punctuation as if Hermia interrupts her, Q1/F3/most modern texts print a period

Before the time I did Lysander see,
Seem'd Athens like[1] a Paradise to mee.   R 146-b

O then, what graces in my Love do dwell,
15   That he hath turn'd a heaven into hell. [2]

Lysander   Helen, to you our mindes we will unfold,
To morrow night, when Phœbe doth behold
Her silver visage, in the watry glasse,
Decking with liquid pearle, the bladed grasse

20   (A time that Lovers flights[3] doth still conceale)
Through Athens gates, have we devis'd to steale.

Hermia   And in the wood, where often you and I,
Upon faint Primrose beds, were wont to lye,

[4] Emptying our bosomes, of their counsell sweld: [5]
25   There my Lysander, and my selfe shall meete,
And thence from Athens turne away our eyes
To seeke new friends and strange companions, [6]

Farwell sweet play-fellow, pray thou for us,
And good lucke grant thee thy Demetrius.

230   Keepe word Lysander we must starve our sight,
From lovers foode, till morrow deepe midnight.

· **[Exit Hermia]**

Lysander   I will my Hermia.
Helena adieu,
As you on him, Demetrius dotes[7] on you.

[Exit Lysander]

235   **Helena**   How happy some, ore othersome can be?
Through Athens I am thought as faire as she.
But what of that?

R 146-b / L 147-c : 1.1.204 - 228

[1] F1/Q2 = 'like', Q1 and most modern texts = 'as'

[2] F1='into hell', Q1/most moderntexts = 'unto a hell'

[3] though most modern texts agree with F1/Qq and print this as 'flights', one interesting gloss = 'slights'

[4] the speech starts with the eighteenth consecutive rhyming couplet in the scene ('I' - 'lye') and ends with another ('us' - 'Demetrius'): the four F1/Qq lines sandwiched in between do not rhyme: however, most modern texts alter 'sweld' to 'sweet', and 'companions' to 'companies' to turn them into two more (couplets 'sweet' - 'meete' and 'eyes' - 'companies')

[5] Ff = 'sweld', most modern texts set 'sweete', to form a couplet with the following 'meete'

[6] F1/Qq = 'strange companions', most modern texts = 'stranger companies'

[7] F1 = 'dotes', Qq and most modern texts = 'dote'

8

Demetrius thinkes not so:
He will not know, what all, but he doth¹ know,
40   And as hee erres, doting on Hermias eyes;
So I, admiring of his qualities:
Things base and vilde, holding no quantity,
Love can transpose to forme and dignity,
Love lookes not with the eyes, but with the minde,
45   And therefore is wing'd Cupid painted blinde.

Nor hath loves minde of any judgement taste:
Wings and no eyes, figure, unheedy haste.

And therefore is Love said to be a childe,
Because in choise he is often² beguil'd,
50   As waggish boyes in game themselves forsweare;
So the boy Love is perjur'd every where.

For ere Demetrius lookt on Hermias eyne,
He hail'd downe oathes that he was onely mine.

And when this³ Haile some heat from Hermia felt,
255 So he dissolv'd, and showres of oathes did melt,
I will goe tell him of faire Hermias flight:
Then to the wood will he, to morrow night
Pursue her; and for his⁴ intelligence,
If I have thankes, it is a deere expence:
260 But heerein meane I to enrich my paine,
To have his sight thither, and backe againe.

[Exit]

**ENTER QUINCE THE CARPENTER, SNUG THE JOYNER, BOTTOME THE
WEAVER, FLUTE THE BELLOWES-MENDER, SNOUT THE TINKER, AND
STARVELING THE TAYLOR**
[Most modern texts create a new scene here, Act One, Scene 2]

Quince   Is all our company heere?

Bottome   You were best to call them generally, man by
                man, according to the scrip.

265 **Quince** Here is the scrowle of every mans name, which
                is thought fit through all Athens, to play in our Enter-
                lude before the Duke and Dutches, on his wedding
                day at night.

L 147 - c : 1.1.228 - 1.2.7

^W¹ F1 = 'doth', Qq and most modern texts = 'do'

^W² F1 = 'is often', Q2 = 'is oft', Q1 and most modern texts = 'is so oft'

^W³ F/Q1 = 'this', Q2 = 'his'

^W⁴ F1 = 'his', Qq and most modern texts = 'this'

Bottome	First, good Peter Quince, say what the play treats
70	on: then read the names of the Actors: and so grow on[1]
	to a point.
Quince	Marry our play is the most lamentable Come-
	dy, and most cruell death of Pyramus and Thisbie.
Bottome	A very good peece of worke I assure you, and a
75	merry.
	Now good Peter Quince, call forth your Actors
	by the scrowle.
	Masters spread your selves.
Quince	Answere as I call you.
80	Nick Bottome the
	Weaver.
Bottome	Ready; name what part I am for, and
	proceed.
Quince	You Nicke Bottome are set downe for Py-
285	ramus.
Bottome	What is Pyramus, a lover, or a tyrant?
Quince	A Lover that kills himselfe most gallantly[2] for
	love.
Bottome	That will aske some teares in the true perfor-
290	ming of it: if I do it, let the audience looke to their eies:
	I will moove stormes; I will condole in some measure.
	To the rest yet, my chiefe humour is for a tyrant.
	I could
	play Ercles rarely, or a part to teare a Cat in, to make all

L 147 - c

> 295 split° the raging Rocks; ° and shivering shocks° shall break
> the locks° of prison gates, ° and Phibbus carre° shall shine
> from farre, ° and make and marre° the foolish Fates. ° [3]

    This

was lofty.
    Now name the rest of the Players.

300

L 147 - c / R 147 - c : 1.2.8 - 39

[1] F1 = 'on', Qq and most modern texts remove the word with no replacement

[2] F1 = 'gallantly', Qq and most modern texts = 'gallant'

[3] F1/Qq all present this passage as prose, most modern texts lay it out according to its rhyming pattern,
as shown by the symbols °: one reading of the source text could be that Bottome is not completely
comfortable with (perhaps is even inventing) the doggerel - certainly it is not presented as accomplished
and polished speech; the modern restructuring presents the material as 'pure' verse which it presumes
Bottome could handle with ease

		This
		is Ercles vaine, a tyrants vaine: a lover is more condo-ling.
	Quince	Francis Flute the Bellowes-mender.
305	**Flute**	Heere Peter Quince.
	Quince	[1] You must take Thisbie on you.
	Flute	What is Thisbie, a wandring Knight?
	Quince	It is the Lady that Pyramus must love.
	Flute	Nay faith, let not mee play a woman, I have a
310		beard comming.
	Quince	That's all one, you shall play it in a Maske, and you may speake as small as you will.
	Bottome	And I may hide my face, let me play Thisbie too: Ile speake in a monstrous little voyce; Thisne, Thisne, ah
315		Pyramus my lover deare, thy Thisbie deare, and Lady deare.
	Quince	No no, you must play Pyramus, and Flute, you Thisby.
	Bottome	Well, proceed.
320	**Quince**	Robin Starveling the Taylor.
	Starveling	Heere Peter Quince.
	Quince	Robin Starveling, you must play Thisbies mother?
		Tom Snowt, the Tinker. [2]
325	**Snout**	Heere Peter Quince.
	Quince	You, Pyramus father; my self, Thisbies father; Snugge the Joyner, you the Lyons part: and I hope there[3] is a play fitted.

R 147 · c : 1.2.40 - 65

[W][1] F1/Q2 print no extra words, Q1 and most modern texts add 'Flute'

[LS][2] arguing that the unusual Ff setting of a separate line for this short sentence stems from the fact that in Q1 this line starts a new page, most modern texts add it to the previous line; if the Ff setting were to stand it might imply some brief hesitation before Quince continues

[W][3] F1 = 'there', Qq and most modern texts = 'here'

Snug	Have you the Lions part written? pray you if [1]	
30	be, give it me, for I am slow of studie.	

Quince	You may doe it extemporie, [2] for it is nothing but roaring.

Bottome	Let mee play the Lyon too, I will roare that I
35	will doe any mans heart good to heare me.

I will roare,
that I will make the Duke say, Let him roare againe, let
him roare againe.

Quince	If [3] you should doe it too terribly, you would
40	fright the Dutchesse and the Ladies, that they would shrike, and that were enough to hang us all.

All	That would hang us every mothers sonne.

Bottome	I graunt you friends, if that [4] you should
345	fright the Ladies out of their Wittes, they would have no more discretion but to hang us: but I will ag-gravate my voyce so, that I will roare you as gently as any sucking Dove; I will roare [5] and 'twere any Nightin-gale.

Quince	You can play no part but Piramus, for Pira-	R 147 - c
350	mus is a sweet-fac'd man, a proper man as one shall see in a summers day; a most lovely Gentleman-like man, ther-fore you must needs play Piramus.	

Bottome	Well, I will undertake it.

What beard were I
best to play it in?

355 **Quince**	Why, what you will.

Bottome	I will discharge it, in either your straw-colour beard, your orange tawnie beard, your purple in graine beard, or your French-crowne colour'd [6] beard, your per-fect [7] yellow.

R 147 - c / L 148 - b : 1.2.66 - 96

ADD [1] Qq/F2/most modern texts add 'it'

W [2] F1/Q2 = 'extemporie', Q1 and most modern texts = 'extempore'

W [3] F1 = 'If', Qq and most modern texts = 'And'

W [4] F1 = 'that', Qq and most modern texts omit the word

W [5] F1 prints no word, Qq and most modern texts add 'you'

W [6] F1 = 'colour'd', Qq and most modern texts = 'colour'

W [7] Q1/most modern texts = 'perfit', Ff = 'perfect'

Quince	Some of your French Crownes have no haire
	at all, and then you will play bare-fac'd.
	But masters here
	are your parts, and I am to intreat you, request you, and
	desire you, to con them by too morrow night: and meet
	me in the palace wood, a mile without the Towne, by
	Moone-light, there we will [1] rehearse: for if we meete in
	the Citie, we shalbe dog'd with company, and our devi-
	ses knowne.
	In the meane time, I wil draw a bil of pro-
	perties, such as our play wants.
	I pray you faile me not.
Bottome	We will meete, and there we may rehearse
	more [2] obscenely and couragiously.
	Take paines, be per-
	fect, adieu.
Quince	At the Dukes oake we meete.
Bottome	Enough, hold or cut bow-strings.

[Exeunt]

---

[1] F1/Q2 = 'we will', Q1 and most modern texts = 'will we'
[2] F1/Q2 = 'more', Q1 and most modern texts = 'most'

Actus Secundus

ENTER A FAIRIE AT ONE DOORE, AND ROBIN GOOD-
FELLOW [1] AT ANOTHER

Robin   [2] **How now spirit, whether[3] wander you** ?

Fairie   Over hil, over dale, ° through[4] bush, through briar, ° [5]
             Over parke, over pale, ° through flood, through fire, °
             I do wander everie where, ° swifter then ÿ [6] Moons sphere; °
             And I serve the Fairy Queene, ° to dew her orbs upon the green .[†] °

             The Cowslips tall, her pensioners bee,
             In their gold coats, spots you see,
             Those be Rubies, Fairie favors,
             In those freckles, live their savors,
             I must go seeke some dew drops heere,
             And hang a pearle in every cowslips eare.

             Farewell thou Lob of spirits, Ile be gon,
             Our Queene and all her Elves come heere anon.

Robin   The King doth keepe his Revels here to night,
             Take heed the Queene come not within his sight,
             For Oberon is passing fell and wrath,
             Because that she, as her attendant, hath

[P][1] throughout the play this character is referred to in two different ways both by the other characters and by
the stage directions/prefixes, perhaps reflecting the two different sides of his nature: 'Robin' (goodfellow)
seems to represent the more mellow mischievous side while 'Pucke' seems to refer to the more troubled
and sometimes darker, almost malevolent aspect of the character: (see the Specific Introduction to this play)

[M][2] the trochaic (reversed iambic/heartbeat) magical/ritual line is shown for the first time in the play (though it
extends beyond its usual length of seven syllables to nine, as if Robin/Pucke was excited or overextending
himself): all such 'magical/ritual' lines will be set in a bolded font in this text

[W][3] F1/Q2 = 'whether', Q1 and most modern texts = 'whither'

[W][4] F1/Q2 = 'through', Q1 and most modern texts = 'thorough' (both spellings yielded either pronunciation
for the Elizabethan: if the short sound - 'through' - is used then the effect is more rushed - see following note)

[ALT/VP][5] F1/Qq print the text as shown, most modern texts print the poetical format as shown by the symbols °:
the modern text version is certainly neater and creates the conventional image of a pretty and delicate
creature: however, the alterations could mask i) how the Fairie is behaving at the top of the scene, (so
rushed as to be unable to control or match Robin/Pucke's magic greeting); ii) the moment of its moving
momentarily into a more ritual/magical form of utterance (which follows this rushed passage) - before iii)
dropping the magical patterns in the realisation of having to go back to work

[AB][6] F1 = 'ÿ', (printed as such because of lack of column width), F3/most modern texts = 'the'

14

		A lovely boy stolne from an Indian King,

A lovely boy stolne from an Indian King,
She never had so sweet a changeling,
20 And jealous Oberon would have the childe
Knight of his traine, to trace the Forrests wilde.

But she (perforce) with-holds the loved boy,
Crownes him with flowers, and makes him all her joy.

And now they never meete in grove, or greene,
25 By fountaine cleere, or spangled star-light sheene,
But they do square, that all their Elves for feare
Creepe into Acorne cups and hide them there.

   Fairie   Either I mistake your shape and making quite,
Or else you are that shrew'd and knavish spirit [1]
30 Cal'd Robin Good-fellow.
                            Are you not hee,
That frights the maidens of the Villagree, [2]
Skim milke, and sometimes labour in the querne,
And bootlesse make the breathlesse huswife cherne,
35 And sometime make the drinke to beare no barme,   L 148 - b
Misleade night-wanderers, laughing at their harme,
Those that Hobgoblin call you, and sweet Pucke,
You do their worke, and they shall have good lucke.

Are not you he?

40 **Robin**   Thou speak'st aright; [3]
I am that merrie wanderer of the night:
I jest to Oberon, and make him smile,
When I a fat and beane-fed horse beguile,
Neighing in likenesse of a silly [4] foale,
45 And sometime lurke I in a Gossips bole,
In very likenesse of a roasted crab:
And when she drinkes, against her lips I bob,
And on her withered dewlop poure the Ale.

The wisest Aunt telling the saddest tale,
50 Sometime for three-foot stoole, mistaketh me,
Then slip I from her bum, downe topples she,
And tailour cries, and fals into a coffe.

L 148 - b / R 148 - b : 2.1.22 - 54

[W] [1] F1/Q2 = 'spirit', Q1 and most modern texts = 'sprite' (both spellings yielded either pronunciation for the Elizabethan)

[W] [2] F1/Q2 = 'Villagree' (three syllables, creating a ten syllable line), Q1 and most modern texts = 'Villageree' (four syllables, creating an eleven syllable line)

[LS] [3] some modern texts join this to the previous line to form a single split verse line: however, the line so created would only be eight syllables long: Q1/Q2 join it to Robin/Pucke's following line thus creating an exuberant 14 or 15 syllable reply: F1 allows for a moment's pause before or after his acknowledgment

[W] [4] F1/Q2 = 'silly', Q1 and most modern texts = 'filly'

15

And then the whole quire hold their hips, and loffe,
And waxen in their mirth, and neeze, and sweare,
55 A merrier houre was never wasted there.

But roome Fairy, heere comes Oberon.

Fairie   And heere my Mistris: → [1]
Would that he were gone.

ENTER THE KING OF FAIRIES [2] AT ONE DOORE WITH HIS TRAINE, AND THE QUEENE [3] AT ANOTHER WITH HERS

Oberon   Ill met by Moone-light→[4]
60   Proud Tytania.

Queene   What, jealous Oberon?
                                    Fairy [5] skip hence,
I have forsworne his bed and companie.

Oberon   Tarrie rash Wanton; am not I thy Lord?

65 **Queene** Then I must be thy Lady: but I know
When thou wast [6] stolne away from Fairy Land,
And in the shape of Corin, sate all day,
Playing on pipes of Corne, and versing love
To amorous Phillida.
70   Why art thou heere
Come from the farthest steepe[7] of India?
But that forsooth the bouncing Amazon
Your buskin'd Mistresse, and your Warrior love,
To Theseus must be Wedded; and you come,
75 To give their bed joy and prosperitie.

[LS 1] Q1 and most modern texts print these two short lines as one complete line: the F1 setting could be used to allow the Fairie a moment of realisation before unsuccessfully attempting to utter an incantation to remove him ('Would that he were gone' is a 'magical' line but only five syllables - and in all the Shakespeare plays a line of magic should be at least seven syllables long to succeed)

[P 2] though described as King of the Fairies in stage directions and occasionally by Robin/Pucke, he is usually called by his given name Oberon in the prefixes, perhaps a sign that he does not always behave as a king

[P 3] throughout the text, she is described as both Queene and Titania, again perhaps referring to two different aspects of her nature

[LS 4] Q1 and most modern texts print these two short lines as one complete line: however, the F1 setting allows for a moment of silence before Oberon greets Titania, and again before she responds

[W 5] F1/Qq = 'Fairy', most modern texts = 'Fairies'

[W 6] F1 = 'wast', Qq and most modern texts = 'hast'

[W 7] F1/Q2 = 'steepe', Q1 and most modern texts = 'steppe'

Oberon	How canst thou thus for shame Tytania,
	Glance at my credite, with Hippolita?
	Knowing I know thy love to Theseus?

Didst thou not [1] leade him through the glimmering night
From Peregenia, [2] whom he ravished?
And make him with faire Eagles [3] breake his faith
With Ariadne, and Atiopa? [4]

Queene	These are the forgeries of jealousie,
	And never since the middle Summers spring
	Met we on hil, in dale, forrest, or mead,
	By paved fountaine, or by rushie brooke,
	Or in the beached margent [5] of the sea,
	To dance our ringlets to the whistling Winde,
	But with thy braules thou hast disturb'd our sport.

Therefore the Windes, piping to us in vaine,
As in revenge, have suck'd up from the sea
Contagious fogges: Which falling in the Land,
Hath everie petty [6] River made so proud,
That they have over-borne their Continents.

The Oxe hath therefore stretch'd his yoake in vaine,
The Ploughman lost his sweat, and the greene Corne
Hath rotted, ere his youth attain'd a beard:
The fold stands empty in the drowned field,
And Crowes are fatted with the murrion flocke,
The nine mens Morris is fild up with mud,
And the queint Mazes in the wanton greene,
For lacke of tread are undistinguishable.

R 148 - b

The humane mortals want their winter heere, [7]
No night is now with hymne or caroll blest;
Therefore the Moone (the governesse of floods)
Pale in her anger, washes all the aire;
That Rheumaticke diseases doe abound.

And through [8] this distemperature, we see

R 148 - b / L 149 - c : 2.1.74 - 106

[w1] F1 = 'thou not', Qq and most modern texts = 'not thou'

[w2] arguing compositor error, some modern texts spell this as 'Peregouna'

[w3] F1/Qq = 'Eagles', most modern texts = 'Aegles'

[w4] F1 = 'Atiopa', Qq and most modern texts = 'Antiopa'

[w5] F1/Qq = 'margent', some modern texts = 'margin'

[w6] F1 = 'petty', Qq and most modern texts = 'pelting'

[w7] F1/Qq = 'heere', most modern texts = 'cheere'

[w8] F1/Q2 = 'through', Q1 and most modern texts = 'thorough'

The seasons alter; hoared[1] headed frosts
Fall in the fresh lap of the crimson Rose,
And on old Hyems chinne[2] and Icie crowne,
And odorous Chaplet of sweet Sommer buds
Is as in mockry set.
     The Spring, the Sommer,
The childing Autumne, angry Winter change
Their wonted Liveries, and the mazed world,
By their increase, now knowes not which is which;
And this same progeny of evills,
Comes[3] from our debate, from our dissention,
We are their parents and originall.

Oberon Do you amend it then, it lies in you,
Why should Titania crosse her Oberon?

I do but beg a little changeling boy,
To be my Henchman.

Queene Set your heart at rest,
The Fairy land buyes not the childe of me,
His mother was a Votresse of my Order,
And in the spiced Indian aire, by night
Full often hath she gossipt by my side,
And sat with me on Neptunes yellow sands,
Marking th'embarked traders on the flood,
When we have laught to see the sailes conceive,
And grow big bellied with the wanton winde:
Which she with pretty and with swimming gate,
Following (her wombe then rich with my yong squire)
Would imitate, and saile upon the Land,
To fetch me trifles, and returne againe,
As from a voyage, rich with merchandize.

But she being mortall, of that boy did die,
And for her sake I doe[4] reare up her boy,
And for her sake I will not part with him.

Oberon How long within this wood intend you stay?

Queene Perchance till after Theseus wedding day.

W 1
 F1/Q2 = 'hoared', Q1 and most modern texts = 'hoary'

W 2
 F1/Qq = 'chinne', most modern texts = 'thin'

LS 3
 some modern texts add 'Comes' to the previous line, thus rendering the source texts' end-of-speech, emotional, two line irregularity (9/11 syllables) back to two normal lines (10/10)

W 4
 F1 = 'I doe', Qq and most modern texts = 'doe I'

	If you will patiently dance in our Round,
	And see our Moone-light revels, goe with us;
	If not, shun me and I will spare your haunts.
Oberon	Give me that boy, and I will goe with thee.
Queene	Not for thy Fairy Kingdome.
	Fairies away:
	We shall chide downe right, if I longer stay.

[Exeunt] [1]

Oberon	Wel, go thy way: thou shalt not from this grove,
	Till I torment thee for this injury.
	My gentle Pucke come hither; thou remembrest
	Since once I sat upon a promontory,
	And heard a Meare-maide on a Dolphins backe,
	Uttering such dulcet and harmonious breath,
	That the rude sea grew civill at her song,
	And certaine starres shot madly from their Spheares,
	To heare the Sea-maids musicke.
Robin as **Pucke** [2]	I remember.
Oberon	That very time I saw †[3] (but thou couldst not)
	Flying betweene the cold Moone and the earth,
	Cupid all arm'd; a certaine aime he tooke
	At a faire Vestall, throned by the West,
	And loos'd his love-shaft smartly from his bow,
	As it should pierce a hundred thousand hearts,
	But I might see young Cupids fiery shaft L 149 - c
	Quencht in the chaste beames of the watry Moone;
	And the imperiall Votresse passed on,
	In maiden meditation, fancy free.
	Yet markt I where the bolt of Cupid fell.
	It fell upon a little westerne flower;
	Before, milke-white; now purple with loves wound,
	And maidens call it, Love in idlenesse.
	Fetch me that flower; the hearb I shew'd thee once,
	The juyce of it, on sleeping eye-lids laid,
	Will make or man or woman madly dote
	Upon the next live creature that it sees.

L 149 - c / R 149 - c : 2.1.140 - 172

SD [1] most modern texts expand the stage direction, explaining that it is the Queene and her train that leave (though the exit of Oberon's attendants is never shown)

P [2] having been named as Pucke during Oberon's speech, Robin is now referred to as Pucke in the prefix too

W [3] F1/Q2 = 'say', Q1 and most modern texts = 'saw'

Fetch me this hearbe, and be thou heere againe,
Ere the Leviathan can swim a league.

Pucke	Ile put a girdle ¹ about the earth,° in forty mi- nutes.
Oberon	Having once this juyce,° ²

Ile watch Titania, when she is asleepe,
And drop the liquor of it in her eyes:
The next thing when³ she waking lookes upon,
(Be it on Lyon, Beare, or Wolfe, or Bull,
On medling Monkey, or on busie Ape)
Shee shall pursue it, with the soule of love.

And ere I take this charme off from⁴ her sight,
(As I can take it with another hearbe)
Ile make her render up her Page to me.

But who comes heere?
I am invisible,
And I will over-heare their conference.

ENTER DEMETRIUS, HELENA FOLLOWING HIM

Demetrius   I love thee not, therefore pursue me not,
Where is Lysander, and faire Hermia?

The one Ile stay, the other stayeth⁵ me.

Thou toldst me they were stolne into this wood;
And heere am I, and wood within this wood,
Because I cannot meet my Hermia
Hence, get thee gone, and follow me no more.

Helena   You draw me, you hard-hearted Adamant;
But yet you draw not Iron, for my heart
Is true as steele.
Leave you your power to draw,
And I shall have no power to follow you.

Demetrius   Do I entice you? do I speake you faire?

R 149 · c : 2.1.173 - 199

ADD/LS ¹ F1/Q2 no extra word, Q1 and most modern texts add 'roúd' ('round'), and an exit for Pucke/Robin

LS ² Qq/F1 print Pucke/Robin's exit speech as an overly long (14 syllables) exuberance: most modern
texts share it with the next line

W ³ F1/Q2 = 'when', Q1 and most modern texts = 'then'

W ⁴ F1/Q2 = 'off from', Q1 and most modern texts = 'from off'

W ⁵ F1/Qq = 'stay' and 'stayeth', most modern texts = 'slay' and 'slayeth'

Or rather doe I not in plainest truth,
Tell you I doe not, nor¹ I cannot love you?

Helena And even for that doe I love thee² the more;
I am your spaniell, and Demetrius,
The more you beat me, I will fawne on you.

Use me but as your spaniell; spurne me, strike me,
Neglect me, lose me; onely give me leave
(Unworthy as I am) to follow you.

What worser place can I beg in your love,
(And yet a place of high respect with me)
Then to be used as you doe³ your dogge.

Demetrius Tempt not too much the hatred of my spirit,
For I am sicke when I do looke on thee.

Helena And I am sicke when I looke not on you.

Demetrius You doe impeach your modesty too much,
To leave the Citty, and commit your selfe
Into the hands of one that loves you not,
To trust the opportunity of night,
And the ill counsell of a desert place,
With the rich worth of your virginity.

Helena Your vertue is my priviledge: for that
It is not night when I doe see your face.

Therefore I thinke I am not in the night,
Nor doth this wood lacke worlds of company,
For you in my respect are all †⁴ the world.

Then how can it be said I am alone,
When all the world is heere to looke on me?

Demetrius Ile run from thee, and hide me in the brakes,
And leave thee to the mercy of wilde beasts.

R 149 - c

ᵂ ¹ F1 and most modern texts = 'nor', Qq = 'not', but it is very important not to reject the Qq reading out of hand: one of the problems in the play is, when the lovers' entanglement is finally resolved, how easily Demetrius accepts Helena: however, if Qq reading stands, his telling her 'I doe not, NOT I cannot love you' and playing the explanation to the full, can help explain his switch from his besotted worship of Hermia back to his rightful place with Helena as something much more than just the convenience of magic

ᵂ ² F1/Q2 = 'thee', Q1 and most modern texts = 'you'

ᵂ ³ F1 shows no extra word, Qq and most modern texts add the word 'use': F1's reading is possible, treating 'used' at the start of the line as a two syllable word (thus emphasising the suggested action even more)

ᵂ ⁴ F1 = 'nll', Qq/F2/most modern texts = 'all'

21

Helena		The wildest hath not such a heart as you;
		Runne when you will, the story shall be chang'd:
40		Apollo flies, and Daphne holds the chase;
		The Dove pursues the Griffin, the milde Hinde
		Makes speed to catch the Tyger.

                          Bootlesse speede,
When cowardise pursues, and valour flies.

45   **Demetrius**   I will not stay thy questions, let me go;
                           Or if thou follow me, doe not beleeve,
                           But I shall doe thee mischiefe in the wood.

Helena   I, in the Temple, in the Towne, and [1] Field
50   You doe me mischiefe.

                            Fye Demetrius,
Your wrongs doe set a scandall on my sexe:
We cannot fight for love, as men may doe;
We should be woo'd, and were not made to wooe.

I [2] follow thee, and make a heaven of hell,
55   To die upon the hand I love so well.

[Exit] [3]

Oberon   Fare thee well Nymph, ere he do leave this grove,
                           Thou shalt flie him, and he shall seeke thy love.

[4]   Hast thou the flower there?
                        Welcome wanderer.

ENTER PUCKE

60   **Pucke**   I, there it is.

      Oberon   I pray thee give it me.

                     I know a banke where the wilde time blowes,
Where Oxslips and the nodding Violet growes,
Quite over-cannoped [5] with luscious woodbine,
65   With sweet muske roses, and with Eglantine;

W [1] F1/Q2 = 'and', Q1 and most modern texts = 'the'

W [2] Ff = 'I', Qq/most modern texts = 'Ile'

SD [3] most modern texts suggest both characters exit here, but this need not be so; Demetrius could have left after his last speech, and thus Helena's last speech could be partly to the audience and partly called after him

SD [4] instead of leaving the entry one line later as shown Qq/F1, most modern texts place Pucke/Robin's entry here: however, the entry of the source text allows Oberon to sense his servant's return before it actually happens, thus adding to his appearance of magic powers

W [5] Ff = 'cannoped', Qq/most modern texts = 'cannopi'd' (i.e. 'canopied')

There sleepes Tytania, sometime of the night,
Lul'd in these[1] flowers, with dances and delight:
And there the snake throwes her enammel'd skinne,
Weed wide enough to rap a Fairy in.

And with the juyce of this Ile streake her eyes,
And make her full of hatefull fantasies.

Take thou some of it, and seek through this grove;
A sweet Athenian Lady is in love
With a disdainefull youth: annoint his eyes,
But doe it when the next thing he espies,
May be the Lady.
           Thou shalt know the man,
By the Athenian garments he hath on.
Effect it with some care, that he may prove
More fond on her, then she upon her love;
And looke thou meet me ere the first Cocke crow.

Pucke   Feare not my Lord, your servant shall do so.

[Exit] [2]

ENTER QUEENE OF FAIRIES, WITH HER TRAINE
[Most modern texts create a new scene here, Act Two, Scene 2]

Queene   Come, now a Roundell, and a Fairy song;
Then for the third part of a minute hence,
Some to kill Cankers in the muske rose buds,
Some warre with Reremise, for their leathern wings,
To make my small Elves coates, and some keepe backe
The clamorous Owle that nightly hoots and wonders
At our queint spirits: Sing me now asleepe,
Then to your offices, and let me rest.

FAIRIES SING [3]

You spotted Snakes with double tongue,
Thorny Hedgebogges be not seene,
Newts and blinde wormes do no wrong,
Come not neere our Fairy Queene .

L 150 - c : 2.1.253 - 2.2.12

W 1 F1/Qq = 'these', some modern texts = 'those'

SD 2 most modern texts add to the exit that they go in different directions

M 3 apart from the first line, the whole song is written in the magical/ritual pattern (the seven syllables
reversed iambic/reversed heartbeat trochaic form) as if the Fairies were indeed putting a spell on the area:
in addition to being italicised (as are all song lines) these 'magical' lines will be bolded for quick recognition

SPD 4 F1/Qq do not assign this to a single character but set the general direction at the top of the song, 'Fairies
Sing': most modern texts give the first sentence to a '1st. Fairy' and assign the next two to the Fairy chorus

5

00

05

10

315

Philomele with melodie,
Sing in your[1] sweet Lullaby.

L 150 - c

Lulla, lulla, lullaby, lulla, lulla, lullaby,
Never harme,° nor spell, nor charme ° [2]
Come our lovely Lady nye,
So good night with Lullaby.

2nd Fairy [3]   *Weaving Spiders come not heere,*
Hence you long leg'd Spinners, hence :
Beetles blacke approach not neere ;
Worme nor Snayle doe no offence .

[4]   *Philomele with melody, &c*

1st. Fairy   *Hence away, now all is well ;*
One aloofe, stand Centinell . [5] [6]

[Shee sleepes] [7]
ENTER OBERON

Oberon   [8] **What thou seest when thou dost wake,**
Doe it for thy true Love take :
Love and languish for his sake .

Be it Ounce, or Catte, or Beare,
Pard, or Boare with bristled haire .

In thy eye that shall appeare,
When thou wak'st, it is thy deare,
Wake when some vile thing is neere . [9]

ENTER LISANDER AND HERMIA

L 150 - c / R 150 - c : 2.2.13 - 34

[W][1] Ff = 'your', Qq = 'our'

[LS][2] because of the rhyme scheme some modern texts split this line in two as shown: Qq/Ff set it as one

[P][3] F1 = 2nd. Fairy, Qq and most modern texts = 1st. Fairy

[P][4] F1/Qq = 1st. or 2nd. Fairy (according to footnote #3 above), most modern texts = Chorus

[SPD][5] though F1/Qq print these two lines in the same style as the song, most modern texts print them as
normal speech: whichever form is chosen, the lines continue the magic/ritual pattern as before

[SD][6] most modern texts add stage directions here for one Fairy to remain while the others quietly leave

[SD][7] this direction first appears in F1: most modern texts assume it is the Queene who sleeps and say so in
their revised stage directions: however, Titania could well have been charmed asleep during the song and
it is whichever Fairy has stayed 'as Centinell' that falls asleep

[SD][8] most modern texts suggest that somewhere during the magic speech Oberon pours the juice into Titania's eye:
for ease of recognition the 'magic' lines will be bolded and centred [this does not occur in Qq/Ff]

[SD][9] most modern texts add a stage direction here for Oberon's exit

	Lysander	Faire love, you faint with wandring in ÿ [1] woods, [2]
		And to speake troth I have forgot our way:
		Wee'll rest us Hermia, if you thinke it good,
		And tarry for the comfort of the day.
20	**Hermia**	Be it so Lysander; finde you out a bed,
		For I upon this banke will rest my head. [3]
	Lysander	One turfe shall serve as pillow for us both,
		One heart, one bed, two bosomes, and one troth.
	Hermia	Nay good Lysander, for my sake my deere
25		Lie further off yet, doe not lie so neere.
	Lysander	O take the sence sweet, of my innocence,
		Love takes the meaning, in loves conference,
		I meane that my heart unto yours is knit,
		So that but one heart can you [4] make of it.
330		Two bosomes interchanged [5] with an oath,
		So then two bosomes, and a single troth.
		Then by your side, no bed-roome me deny,
		For lying so, Hermia, I doe not lye.
	Hermia	Lysander riddles very prettily;
335		Now much beshrew my manners and my pride,
		If Hermia meant to say, Lysander lied.
		But gentle friend, for love and courtesie
		Lie further off, in humane modesty,
		Such separation, as may well be said,
340		Becomes a vertuous batchelour, and a maide,
		So farre be distant, and good night sweet friend;
		Thy love nere alter, till thy sweet life end.
	Lysander	Amen, amen, to that faire prayer, say I,
		And then end life, when I end loyalty:
345		Heere is my bed, sleepe give thee all his rest. [6]
	Hermia	With halfe that wish, the wishers eyes be prest.

AB[1] F1 = 'ÿ', (printed as such because of lack of column width), F2/most modern texts = 'the'

W[2] F1/Q2 = 'woods', Q1 and most modern texts = 'wood'

SD[3] some modern texts specify that she lies down now

W[4] F1/Q2 = 'can you', Q1 and most modern texts = 'wee can'

W[5] F1 = 'interchanged', Qq and most modern texts = 'interchained'

SD[6] most modern texts specify that this is when Lysander lies down, some distance from Hermia

ENTER PUCKE
[They sleepe]

Pucke   Through the Forrest have I gone,
                            But Athenian finde[1] I none,

350   One[2] whose eyes I might approve
                            This flowers force in stirring love.

Night and silence : who is heere?

                            Weedes of Athens he doth weare :
                            This is he (my master said)
                            Despised the Athenian maide :

355   <center>And heere the maiden sleeping sound,[3]</center>   R 150 - c
                            On the danke and durty ground .[4]

                            Pretty soule, she durst not lye
                            Neere this lacke-love, this kill-curtesie .

                            Churle, upon thy eyes I throw [5]

360   All the power this charme doth owe :
                            When thou wak'st, let love forbid
                            Sleepe his seate on thy eye-lid .

                            So awake when I am gone :
                            For I must now to Oberon . [6]

[Exit]
ENTER DEMETRIUS AND HELENA RUNNING

365   **Helena**   Stay, though thou kill me, sweete Demetrius.

        Demetrius   I charge thee hence, and do not haunt me thus.

        Helena   O wilt thou darkling leave me? do not so.

        Demetrius   Stay on thy perill, I alone will goe.

[Exit Demetrius] [7]

W [1] F1/Q2 = 'finde', Q1 and most modern texts = 'found'

W [2] F1/Q2 = 'One', Q1 and most modern texts = 'On'

M/STRUCT [3] Pucke/Robin's magic/ritual pattern momentarily slips when he sees the human female: this change in speaking style when faced with women is a pattern that is repeated later, Act Three, pages 55-6 this script: for easier recognition the magic speech has been centred on the page, not an F1 practice

PCT [4] the punctuation mark is very faint in F1; Q2/F2 print a period

SD [5] most modern texts specify he puts the juice in Lysander's eye now - though it could really occur anywhere in this sentence

M [6] once more his 'magic' speech pattern breaks, as he mentions Oberon

UE [7] set on a separate line rather than to the side of dialogue, this escape-exit may be more important than usual

26

Helena	O I am out of breath, in this fond chace,
370	The more my prayer, the lesser is my grace,
	Happy is Hermia, wheresoere she lies;
	For she hath blessed and attractive eyes.

How came her eyes so bright?
                  Not with salt teares. [1]

375   If so, my eyes are oftner washt then hers.

No, no, I am as ugly as a Beare;
For beasts that meete me, runne away for feare,
Thereforc no marvaile, though Demetrius
Doe as a monster, flie my presence thus.

380   What wicked and dissembling glasse of mine,
Made me compare with Hermias sphery eyne?

But who is here?
              Lysander on the ground;
Deade or asleepe?
385   I see no bloud, no wound,
Lysander, if you live, good sir awake.

Lysander   [2] And run through fire I will for thy sweet sake.

Transparent Helena, nature her shewes art,[3]
That through thy bosome makes me see thy heart.

390   Where is Demetrius? oh how fit a word
Is that vile name, to perish on my sword!

Helena   Do not say so Lysander, say not so:
What though he love your Hermia?
                     Lord, what though?
395   Yet Hermia still loves you; then be content. [4]

Lysander   Content with Hermia?
               No, I do repent
The tedious minutes I with her have spent.

Not Hermia, but Helena now [5] I love;
400   Who will not change a Raven for a Dove?

L 151 - d : 2.2.88 - 114

---

[1] F1 sets a blurred mark, F2-4 a period: Qq sets a comma: most modern texts set a semi-colon

[2] most modern texts add the stage direction that he does awake

[3] F1 = 'nature her shewes art', F2 = 'nature here shewes art', Qq = 'nature shewes art', some modern texts = 'nature shows her art'

[4] this could be one long sentence, or as many as three short ones

[5] F1/Q2 = 'now', Q1 and most modern texts print no word here

The will of man is by his reason sway'd:
And reason saies you are the worthier Maide.

Things growing are not ripe untill their season;
So I being yong, till now ripe not to reason,
And touching now the point of humane skill,
Reason becomes the Marshall to my will,
And leades me to your eyes, where I orelooke
Loves stories, written in Loves richest booke.

Helena   Wherefore was I to this keene mockery borne?

When at your hands did I deserve this scorne?

Ist not enough, ist not enough, yong man,
That I did never, no nor never can,
Deserve a sweete looke from Demetrius eye,
But you must flout my insufficiency?

Good troth you do me wrong (good-sooth you do)
In such disdainfull manner, me to wooe.

But fare you well; perforce I must confesse,
I thought you Lord of more true gentlenesse.

Oh, that a Lady of one man refus'd,
Should of another therefore be abus'd.

[Exit]

Lysander   She sees not Hermia: Hermia sleepe thou there,
And never maist thou come Lysander neere;
For as a surfeit of the sweetest things
The deepest loathing to the stomacke brings:
Or as the heresies that men do leave,
Are hated most of those that[1] did deceive:
So thou, my surfeit, and my heresie,
Of all be hated; but the most of me;
And all my powers addresse your love and might,
To honour Helen, and to be her Knight.

L 151 - d

[Exit]

Hermia   [2] Helpe me Lysander, helpe me; do thy best
To plucke this crawling serpent from my brest.

Aye me, for pitty; what a dreame was here?

L 151 - d / R 151 - d : 2.2.115 - 147

[1] F1 = 'that', Qq and most modern texts = 'they'

[2] most modern texts explain she awakes after Lysander's exit, one contemporary director suggests 'as from a nightmare'

Lysander looke, how I do quake with feare:
35   Me-thought a serpent eate my heart away,
And yet [1] sat smiling at his cruell prey.

Lysander, what remoov'd?
                                        Lysander, Lord,
What, out of hearing, gone?
40   No sound, no word?

Alacke where are you? speake and if you heare:
Speake of all loves; I sound almost with feare.

No, then I well perceive you are not nye,
Either death or you Ile finde immediately.

[Exit]

R 151 - d : 2.2.148 - 156

---

[1] F1 = 'yet', Qq and most modern texts = 'you'

Actus Tertius

ENTER THE CLOWNES [1]

Bottome	Are we all met?
Quince	Pat, pat, and here's a marvailous convenient place for our rehearsall. This greene plot shall be our stage, this hauthorne brake our tyring house, and we will do it in action, as we will do it before the Duke.
Bottome	Peter quince?
Quince as **Peter**	What saist thou, bully Bottome?
Bottome	There are things in this Comedy of Piramus and Thisby, that will never please. First, Piramus must draw a sword to kill himselfe; which the Ladies cannot abide. How answere you that?
Snout	Berlaken, a parlous feare.
Starveling	I beleeve we must leave the killing out, when all is done.
Bottome	Not a whit, I have a device to make all well. Write me a Prologue, and let the Prologue seeme to say, we will do no harme with our swords, and that Pyramus is not kill'd indeede: and for the more better assurance, tell them, that I Piramus am not Piramus, but Bottome the Weaver; this will put them out of feare.
˙Quince˙	Well, we will have such a Prologue, and it shall be written in eight and sixe.
Bottome	No, make it two more, let it be written in eight and eight.

SD [1]
 some modern texts add that Titania is sleeping nearby

Snout	Will not the Ladies be afear'd of the Lyon?	
Starveling	I feare it, I promise you.	
Bottome	Masters, you ought to consider with your selves,[1] to	
30	bring in (God shield us) a Lyon among Ladies, is a most	
	dreadfull thing.	
	For there is not a more fearefull wilde	
	foule then your Lyon living: and wee ought to looke	
	to it. [2]	
35 **Snout**	Therefore another Prologue must tell he is not	
	a Lyon.	
Bottome	Nay, you must name his name, and halfe his face	
	must be seene though the Lyons necke, and he himselfe	
	must speake through, saying thus, or to the same defect;	
40	Ladies, or faire Ladies, I would wish you, or I would	R 151 - d
	request you, or I would entreat you, not to feare, not to	
	tremble: my life for yours.	
	If you thinke I come hither	
	as a Lyon, it were pitty of my life.	
45	No, I am no such	
	thing, I am a man as other men are; and there indeed let	
	him name his name, and tell them[3] plainly hee is Snug the	
	joyner.	
Quince	Well, it shall be so; but there is two hard	
50	things, that is, to bring the Moone-light into a cham-	
	ber: for you know, Piramus and Thisby meete by Moone-	
	light.	
Snout [4]	Doth the Moone shine that night wee play our	
	play?	
55 **Bottome**	A Calendar, a Calendar, looke in the Almanack,	
	finde out Moone-shine, finde out Moone-shine.	

ENTER PUCKE [5]

R 151 - d / 152 - d : 3.1.27 - 54

[W][1] F1 = 'your selves', Qq and most modern texts = 'your selfe'

[W][2] F1/Q2 = 'to it', Q1 and most modern texts = 'toote' (i.e. to't)

[W][3] F1 = 'him', Qq and most modern texts = 'them'

[P][4] F2 is the first text to specify who speaks this line, F1/Qq just assign the prefix 'Sn.' which could apply to either Snug or Snout

[SDP][5] see the Specific Introduction to this play for a detailed discussion of his entry as Pucke here and another as the character Robin (with no exit in between) some 22 First Folio lines later: some modern texts disavow this entry completely, others keep it and turn the second entry (see footnote #2 next page) into an aside

Quince	Yes, it doth shine that night.
Bottome	Why then may you leave a casement of the great chamber window (where we play) open, and the Moone may shine in at the casement.
Quince	I, or else one must come in with a bush of thorns and a lanthorne, and say he comes to disfigure, or to present the person of Moone-shine.

Then there is another thing, we must have a wall in the great Chamber; for Piramus and Thisby (saies the story) did talke through the chinke of a wall.

Snout	You can never bring in a wall.

What say you Bottome?

Bottome	Some man or other must present wall, and let him have some Plaster, or some Lome, or some rough cast about him, to signifie wall; or[1] let him hold his fingers thus; and through that cranny, shall Piramus and Thisby whisper.
Quince	If that may be, then all is well.

Come, sit downe every mothers sonne, and rehearse your parts.

Piramus, you begin; when you have spoken your speech, enter into that Brake, and so every one according to his cue.

ENTER ROBIN [2]

˙**Robin**˙	What hempen home-spuns have we swaggering here, So neere the Cradle of the Faierie Queene?

What, a Play toward?

Ile be an auditor, An Actor too perhaps, if I see cause.

Quince	Speake Piramus: Thisby stand forth.

[W][1] Qq/Ff = 'or', some modern texts = 'and'

[SD][2] see footnote #5 on the preceding page, and the Specific Introduction to this play: modern texts either make this the first entry for Pucke/Robin, or allow the first entry and turn this direction into an aside

{Bottome as} **Piramus** [1]

Thisby, the flowers of odious savors sweete. [2]

90 **Quince** Odours, odours. [3]

{Bottome as} **Piramus**

Odours savors sweete,
So hath thy breath, my dearest Thisby deare.
But harke, a voyce: stay thou but here a while,
And by and by I will to thee appeare.

[Exit Piramus] [4]

95 Robin as
Pucke A stranger Piramus, then ere plaid here. [5] [6]

Flute as
Thisbe [7] Must I speake now?

'Peter' [8] I marry must you.
For you must understand he
goes but to see a noyse that he heard, and is to come a-
00 gaine.

{Flute as} **Thisby**

Most radiant Piramus, most Lilly white of hue,
Of colour like the red rose on triumphant bryer,
Most brisky [9] Juvenall, and eke most lovely Jew, [10]
As true as truest horse, that yet would never tyre,
05 Ile meete thee Piramus, at Ninnies toombe.

Peter Ninus toombe man: why, you must not speake
that yet; that you answere to Piramus: you speake all
your part at once, cues and all.
Piramus enter, your cue is
110 past; it is never tyre.

P[1] as the rehearsal starts F1/Qq rename him Piramus, most modern texts still call him Bottome,

ALT[2] for clarity the Mechanical's play will be shown in a smaller font (though this is not done so in Ff/Qq)

W[3] so many reinterpretations are offered for this line, see Brooks' The Arden edition, A Midsummer Nights Dream, op. cit., pages 155-158: Q1 = 'Odors, odorous.', F = 'Odours, odours.', some modern texts = 'Odors, odious.', others = 'Odious? Odorous!'

P[4] F1 specifically states Bottome exits as Piramus, most modern texts simply give an exit for Bottome

P[5] Qq assign this line to Quince

SD[6] most modern texts give Robin/Pucke the direction to exit after Bottome

P[7] Flute is now renamed Thisby by F1/Qq, and as the rehearsal process continues so F1 elongates the 'i' to 'y', i.e. Thysbe (perhaps Flute is growing in confidence): modern texts keep the prefix Flute

P[8] as Quince starts directing and coaching in earnest, F1 renames him Peter, perhaps suggesting he is taking a kinder, gentler approach to Flute: Q1 and most modern texts still refer to him as Quince

W[9] Qq/Ff/most modern texts = 'brisky', one gloss = 'bristly'

W[10] arguing that 'Jew' was Elizabethan slang for 'juvenile', many modern texts alter 'Jew' to 'Juve'

{Flute}	O,	

    {Flute as} **Thisby**

         as true and truest horse, that yet would never
         tyre: [1]

                                           L 152 - d

    {Bottome as} **Piramus** [2]

         If I were faire, Thisby I were onely thine. [3]

Peter   O monstrous.
                  O strange.
                         We are hanted; [4] pray
masters, flye masters, helpe.

THE CLOWNES ALL EXIT [5]

Pucke   Ile follow you, Ile leade you about a Round,
          Through bogge, through bush, through brake, through bryer, [†]
          Sometime a horse Ile be, sometime a hound:
          A hogge, a headlesse beare, sometime a fire,
          And neigh, and barke, and grunt, and rore, and burne,
          Like horse, hound, hog, beare, fire, at every turne. .

[Exit]
ENTER PIRAMUS WITH THE ASSE HEAD [6]

Bottome   Why do they run away?
                     This is a knavery of
them to make me afeard.

[Enter Snowt] [7]

Snout   O Bottom, thou art chang'd; What doe I see on
          thee?

L 152 - d / R 152 - d : 3.1.103 - 115

[SD 1] most modern texts reposition to here the F1 stage direction of eight lines later (that Bottome enters with an ass-head on his shoulders) - see footnote #6 below: most add that Robin/Pucke accompanies, follows, or even leads him in: also F4/Qq/most modern texts set a period, F1-3 set a colon as if Bottome's entry almost interrupts Flute/Thisbe

[P 2] there is much theatrical potential in the fact that Bottome, despite the transformation, is still described as Piramus

[RCT 3] one splendid modern gloss repunctuates the line, 'If I were, faire Thisby, I were only thine.'

[W 4] F1 = 'hanted', Qq and most modern texts = 'haunted'

[UE 5] this exit should draw extra attention (being printed unusually on a separate line, not alongside the text)

[SD 6] some modern texts remove this direction and place it eight lines earlier (see footnote #1, above): others keep it, and have Bottome/Piramus follow after when all the other Clownes exit: notice, he is still called Piramus in F1's stage direction to enter, but something in him would seem to alter on-stage after the entry and he is called Bottome by the time he speaks

[UE 7] with the entry being unusually set alongside the text instead of being centred on a separate line, it would seem Snout does not wish to draw attention to himself: also with F1 specifically giving the entry to Snout, the question of to whom does the following F1/Qq prefix of Sn. belong is answered, at least in F1

Bottome	What do you see? You see an Asse-head of your owne, do you?

¹ **ENTER PETER QUINCE**

Peter	Blesse thee Bottome, blesse thee; thou art transla- ted.

[Exit]

Bottome	I see their knavery; this is to make an asse of me, to fright me if they could; but I will not stirre from this place, do what they can. I will walke up and downe here, and I will sing that they shall heare I am not a- fraid.

> ² *The Woosell ³ cocke, so blacke of hew,*
> *With Orenge-tawny bill.*
>
> *The Throstle, with his note so true,*
> *The Wren and ⁴ little quill.*

Queene as **Titania** ^{5 6}	What Angell wakes me from my flowry bed?
Bottome	*The Finch, the Sparrow, and the Larke,* *The plainsong Cuckow gray;* *Whose note full many a man doth marke,* *And dares not answere nay.*
	For indeede, who would set his wit to so foolish a bird? Who would give a bird the lye, though he cry Cuckow, never so?
Titania	I pray thee gentle mortall, sing againe, Mine eare is much enamored of thy note; On the first view to say, to sweare I love thee. ⁷

R 152 - d : 3.1.116 - 141

^{SD} ₁ prior to Quince's entry, most modern texts give an exit for Snout

^{SD/SD} ₂ most modern texts add the direction that he starts to sing, and continues after Titania's line

^W ₃ F1/Qq = 'Woosell', most modern texts = 'Ousel'

^W ₄ F1 = 'and', Qq and most modern texts = 'with'

^P ₅ this is the first time the prefix has referred to her as Titania rather than Queene: (apart from making her fall in love with the first thing seen, how else has the potion affected her personality and behaviour?)

^{SD/A} ₆ most modern texts add two directions, first, she awakes, second the line is an aside: the first is a given, though with the second, the line may be played directly to Bottome who doesn't (or pretends not to) hear

^{LS/ALT} ₇ this line only appears in this position in Q2/F; most modern texts follow Q1 and put it at the end of the speech - though if Titania is truly shaken up by the spell the disoriented F/Q2 reading could still stand

So is mine eye enthralled to thy shape.

And thy faire vertues force (perforce) doth move me.

Bottome   Me-thinkes mistresse, you should have little

60   reason for that: and yet to say the truth, reason and
love keepe little company together, now-adayes.

The more the pittie, that some honest neighbours will
not make them friends.
                              Nay, I can gleeke upon occa-
sion.

165   **Titania**   Thou art as wise, as thou art beautifull.

Bottome   Not so neither: but if I had wit enough to get
out of this wood, I have enough to serve mine owne
turne.

Titania   Out of this wood, do not desire to goe,

170   Thou shalt remaine here, whether thou wilt or no.

I am a spirit of no common rate:
The Summer still doth tend upon my state,
And I doe love thee; therefore goe with me,
Ile give thee Fairies to attend on thee;

175   And they shall fetch thee Jewels from the deepe,
And sing, while thou on pressed flowers dost sleepe:
And I will purge thy mortall grossenesse so,
That thou shalt like an airie spirit go.

**ENTER PEASE-BLOSSOME, COBWEB, MOTH, MUSTARD-
SEEDE,** [1] **AND FOURE FAIRIES**

Fairies	Ready; ° and I, ° and I, ° and I, ° Where shall we go? [2]	R 152 - d

180   **Titania**   Be kinde and curteous to this Gentleman,
Hop in his walkes, and gambole in his eies,
Feede him with Apricocks, and Dewberries,
With purple Grapes, greene Figs, and Mulberries,
The honie-bags steale from the humble Bees,

185   And for night-tapers crop their waxen thighes,

R 152 - d / L 151* - d : 3.1.142 - 169

SD/COMP/P [1]
virtually all modern texts follow Q1 and assign the four names as a line of dialogue to Titania: Q1 then
printed on a separate line, presumably as a stage direction, 'Enter Foure Fairies': unfortunately, Elizabethan
printing conventions put both real names and stage directions in the same style of italic type; as a
consequence in this case later texts muddled dialogue (the real names) with stage directions - hence
F1's confusion; only four Fairies should enter, those Titania calls in by name

P [2]
F1/Qq assign the line to all the Fairies, some modern texts follow suit, others split it up in various
permutations - the most popular being shown with the symbol °, (all four speak 'Where shall we go?')

And light them at the fierie-Glow-wormes eyes,
To have my love to bed, and to arise:
And plucke the wings from painted Butterflies,
To fan the Moone-beames from his sleeping eies.

90   Nod to him Elves, and doe him curtesies. [1]

1st. Fairy   Haile mortall, haile. [2]

2nd. Fairy   Haile.

3rd. Fairy   Haile.

Bottome   I cry your worships mercy hartily; I beseech
95   your worships name.

Cobweb   Cobweb.

Bottome   I shall desire you of more acquaintance, good
                    Master Cobweb: if I cut my finger, I shall make bold
                    with you.

00   Your name honest Gentleman?

Pease-Blossome   Pease blossome.

Bottome   I pray you commend mee to mistresse Squash,
                    your mother, and to master Peascod your father.
                                                         Good
05   master Pease-blossome, I shal desire of you[3] more acquain-
                    tance to.
                                Your name I beseech you sir?

Mustard-seede   Mustard-seede.

Pease-blossome   Pease-blossome. [4]

10 **Bottome**   Good master Mustard seede, I know your pati-
                    ence well: that same cowardly gyant-like Oxe-beefe
                    hath devoured many a gentleman of your house.
                                                         I pro-
                    mise you, your kindred hath made my eyes water ere
15   now.

L 151* - d : 3.1.170 - 195

P 1
with the following lines most modern texts call Fairy #1 Pease-blossom, #2 Moth, #3 Mustardseed

P 2
some modern texts give the final 'haile' to Cobweb (who otherwise would not speak in this sequence)

W 3
F1 = 'of you', Qq and most modern texts = 'you of'

COMP/ALT 4
this over-eager repetition by Pease-blossome of his name appears only in F: no modern texts print
it (arguing the line - spoken four lines earlier - was repeated in F1 merely because of compositor error)

                    I desire you more[1] acquaintance, good Master
                    Mustard-seede.

Titania   Come waite upon him, lead him to my bower.

                    The Moone me-thinks, lookes with a watrie eie,
'0   And when she weepes, weepe[2] everie little flower,
                    Lamenting some enforced chastitie.

                    Tye up my lovers[3] tongue, bring him silently.

[Exit]
ENTER KING OF PHARIES, SOLUS
[Most modern texts create a new scene here, Act Three, Scene 2]

Oberon   I wonder if Titania be awak't;
                    Then what it was that next came in her eye,
:5   Which she must dote on, in extremitie.

ENTER PUCKE

                    Here comes my messenger: how now mad spirit,
                    What night-rule now about this gaunted[4] grove?

Pucke   My Mistris with a monster is in love,
                    Neere to her close and consecrated bower,
30   While she was in her dull and sleeping hower,
                    A crew of patches, rude Mechanicals,[†5]
                    That worke for bread upon Athenian stals,
                    Were met together to rehearse a Play,
                    Intended for great Theseus nuptiall day:
35   The shallowest thick-skin of that barren sort,
                    Who Piramus presented, in their sport,
                    Forsooke his Scene, and entred in a brake,[6]
                    When I did him at this advantage take,[7]
                    An Asses nole I fixed on his head.

L 151* - d : 3.1.195 - 3.2.17

[W1] Qq/F1-2 = 'you more', F3 = 'your more', some modern texts = 'you of more'

[W2] F1/Q2 = 'weepe', Q1 and most modern texts = 'weepes'

[W3] F1/Qq = 'lovers', most modern texts = 'love's'

[W4] F1 = 'gaunted', Qq/F2/most modern texts = 'haunted'

[W5] F1 = 'Mcehanicals', F2/Qq/most modern texts = 'Mechanicals'

[RCT6] though Qq/Ff sct a comma, most modern texts have Pucke gather his thoughts here and set a semi-colon

[RCT7] Q1 with a colon, Q2 with a semi-colon, give Pucke more of a flourish just before he tells Oberon of his masterful trick: Ff/most modern texts set a comma

Anon his Thisbie must be answered,
And forth my Mimmick comes: when they him spie,
As Wilde-geese, that the creeping Fowler eye,
Or russed [1]-pated choughes, many in sort
(Rising and cawing at the guns report)
Sever themselves, and madly sweepe the skye: L 151a [2] - d
So at his sight, away his fellowes flye,
And at our stampe, here ore and ore one fals;
He murther cries, and helpe from Athens cals.

Their sense thus weake, lost with their fears thus strong,
Made senselesse things begin to do them wrong.

For briars and thornes at their apparell snatch,
Some sleeves, some hats, from yeelders all things catch,
I led them on in this distracted feare,
And left sweete Piramus translated there:
When in that moment (so it came to passe)
Tytania waked, and straightway lov'd an Asse.

Oberon	This fals out better then I could devise:
	But hast thou yet lacht the Athenians eyes,
	With the love juyce, as I did bid thee doe?
‛Robin˙	I tooke him sleeping (that is finisht to)
	And the Athenian woman by his side,
	That when he wak't, of force she must be eyde.

ENTER DEMETRIUS AND HERMIA

Oberon	Stand close, this is the same Athenian.
Robin	This is the woman, but not this the man.
Demetrius	O why rebuke you him that loves you so?
	Lay breath so bitter on your bitter foe.
Hermia	Now I but chide, but I should use thee worse.
	For thou (I feare) hast given me cause to curse,
	If thou hast slaine Lysander in his sleepe,

> Being ore shooes in bloud, plunge in the deepe,° and kill
> me too:° [3]

L 151* - d / R 151 *- d : 3.2.18 - 49

[W] [1] F1 = 'russed' (though the imprint is faint and could possibly = ruffed), Qq and most modern texts = 'russet'

[COMP] [2] F1/2 mistakenly mark this page as the second #151: if numbered in strict sequence it should be #153

[LS] [3] the F1/Qq printing of the long line (13 or 14 syllables) seems perfectly justified given Hermia's
circumstances: the two line modern lineation (9 or 10/4) 'normalises' a most abnormal moment

The Sunne was not so true unto the day,
As he to me.
         Would he have stollen away,
From sleeping Hermia?
              Ile beleeve as soone
This whole earth may be bord, and that the Moone
May through the Center creepe, and so displease
Her brothers noonetide, with th'Antipodes.

It cannot be but thou hast murdred him,
So should a murtherer[1] looke, so dead, so grim.

Demetrius So should the murderer[2] looke, and so should I,
Pierst through the heart with your stearne cruelty:
Yet you the murderer looks[3] as bright as cleare,
As yonder Venus in her glimmering spheare.

Hermia What's this to my Lysander? where is he?

Ah good Demetrius, wilt thou give him me?

Demetrius I'de[4] rather give his carkasse to my hounds.

Hermia Out dog, out cur, thou driv'st me past the bounds
Of maidens patience.
            Hast thou slaine him then?

Henceforth be never numbred among men.

Oh, once tell true,[5] even for my sake,
Durst thou a[6] lookt upon him being awake?

And hast thou kill'd him sleeping?
           O brave tutch:
Could not a worme, an Adder do so much?

An Adder did it: for with doubler tongue
Then thine (thou serpent) never Adder stung.

Demetrius You spend your passion on a mispri'sd mood,
I am not guiltie of Lysanders blood:
Nor is he dead for ought that I can tell.

R 151* - d : 3.2.50 - 76

[1] F1 = 'mutrherer', Qq/F2/most modern texts = 'murtherer'
[2] F1 = 'murderer', Qq and most modern texts = 'murthered'
[3] F1 = 'looks', Qq and most modern texts = 'looke'
[4] F1/Q2 = 'I'de', Q1 and most modern texts = 'I had' (thus creating an eleven syllable line)
[5] F1/Q2 show no extra text, Q1 and most modern texts repeat 'tell true'
[6] F1 = 'a', Qq and most modern texts = 'have'

| Hermia | I pray thee tell me then that he is well. |

Demetrius And if I could, what should I get therefore?

05 **Hermia** A priviledge, never to see me more;

> And from thy hated presence part I: ° see me no more
> Whether he be dead or no.° 1

[Exit]

Demetrius There is no following her in this fierce vaine,
Here therefore for a while I will remaine.

10 So sorrowes heavinesse doth heavier grow:
For debt that bankrout slip² doth sorrow owe,
Which now in some slight measure it will pay,   R 151a³ - d
If for his tender here I make some stay.

[Lie downe] 4

Oberon What hast thou done?
                              Thou hast mistaken quite
15 And laid the love juyce on some true loves sight:
Of thy misprision, must perforce ensue
Some true love turn'd, and not a false turn'd true.

Robin Then fate ore-rules, that one man holding troth,
20 A million faile, confounding oath on oath.

Oberon About the wood, goe swifter then the winde,
And Helena of Athens looke thou finde.

All fancy sicke she is, and pale of cheere,
With sighes of love, that costs the fresh bloud deare.

25 By some illusion see thou bring her heere,
Ile charme his eyes against she doth⁵ appeare.

R 151ᵉ - d / L 154 - c : 3.2.77 - 99

LS 1 F1/Qq's irregularity (13/7 syllables) allow Hermia to explode before exiting - having also broken a long sequence of rhyming couplets; it also gives Demetrius a moment of stunned silence before he starts to talk: most modern texts regularise the irregular lines (10/11) thus normalising the moment, and maintain the couplets by adding the word 'so' after the new first line, viz. 'And from thy hated presence part I so': this and the earlier Ff/Qq explosion in this scene are vital not only for the development of Hermia's loss of composure, they also help to up the importance of her next entry: it seems a shame that most modern texts have regularised both passages

W 2 F1 = 'slip', Qq = 'slippe' which most modern texts set as 'sleepe'

COMP 3 if accurately numbered, this column should read R153 (see footnote #2, page 39)

SD 4 most modern texts add that Demetrius sleeps, and Oberon and Robin/Pucke come forward

W 5 F1 = 'doth', Qq and most modern texts = 'doe'

41

Robin		I go, I go, looke how I goe, Swifter then arrow from the Tartars bowe.

[Exit]

Oberon   ¹

330

Flower of this purple die,
Hit with Cupids archery,
Sinke in apple of his eye,
When his love he doth espie,
Let her shine as gloriously
As the Venus of the sky .

335

When thou wak'st if she be by,
Beg of her for remedy .

ENTER PUCKE ²

Robin as
Pucke

Captaine of our Fairy band,
Helena is heere at hand,
And the youth, mistooke by me,

340

Pleading for a Lovers fee .

Shall we their fond Pageant see *?*

Lord, what fooles these mortals be *!*

Oberon

Stand aside : the noyse they make,
Will cause Demetrius to awake. ³

345   **Pucke**

Then will two at once wooe one,
That must needs be sport alone :
And those things doe best please me,
That befall preposterously . ⁴

ENTER LYSANDER AND HELENA ⁵

L 154 - c : 3.2.100 - 121

M/SD/STRUCT ₁ during the speech (which is again written in the seven syllable reversed iambic heartbeat pattern
of magic/ritual) most modern texts add a stage direction for Oberon to pour the love juice into
Demetrius' eye

M/P/SD ₂ having exited in disgrace as Robin, the F1/Qq character now successfully returns as Pucke, and
also speaks in the magical/ritual pattern (either a leftover from the magic used to bring Helena hither, or
taking his cue from Oberon)

M ₃ just for this one line does Oberon lose his magical equilibrium (perhaps he realises that, yet again,
Pucke/Robin hasn't quite done what was asked of him - bringing Lysander was not part of Oberon's
request and will only complicate matters even further!)

WM ₄ F1/Q2 = 'preposterously', Q1 and most modern texts = 'prepost'rously' (so keeping the 7 syllable pattern)

SD ₅ for the rest of this scene most modern texts provide numerous suggestions (sometimes unwarranted)
as to who is speaking to whom: this script will only provide 'in-text' directions where F1/Qq do

Lysander	Why should you think ÿ[1] I should wooe in scorn?
350	Scorne and derision never comes[2] in teares:
	Looke when I vow I weepe; and vowes so borne,
	In their nativity all truth appeares.
	How can these things in me, seeme scorne to you?
	Bearing the badge of faith to prove them true.
355 **Helena**	You doe advance your cunning more & more,
	When truth kils truth, O divelish holy fray!
	These vowes are Hermias.
	Will you give her ore?
	Weigh oath with oath, and you will nothing weigh.
360	Your vowes to her, and me, (put in two scales)
	Will even weigh, and both as light as tales.
Lysander	I had no judgement, when to her I swore.
Helena	Nor none in my minde, now you give her ore.
Lysander	Demetrius loves her, and he loves not you.

[Awa{kes}] [3]

365 **Demetrius**	O Helen, goddesse, nimph, perfect, divine,
	To what [4] my love, shall I compare thine eyne!
	Christall is muddy, O how ripe in show,
	Thy lips, those kissing cherries, tempting grow!
	That pure congealed white, high Taurus snow,
370	Fan'd with the Easterne winde, turnes to a crow,
	When thou holdst up thy hand.
	O let me kisse
	This Princesse[5] of pure white, this seale of blisse.
Helena	O spight!
375	O hell!
	I see you are all [6] bent
	To set against me, for your merriment:

L 154 - c : 3.2.122- 146

AB [1] F1/F2 = 'ÿ', (printed as such because of lack of column width), F3/Qq/most modern texts = 'that'

W [2] F1/Q2 = 'comes', Q1 and most modern texts = 'come'

SD [3] the F1 stage direction is simply 'Awa.': most modern texts expand this to 'Demetrius Awakes'

PCT [4] Qq/F2/most modern texts add a comma, F3-4 set a question mark: F1 omits punctuation altogether here, but some copies of the page show a faint comma after the next word ('my')

W [5] F1/Qq = 'Princesse', most modern texts = 'pureness'

W [6] F1 = 'are all', Qq and most modern texts = 'all are'

If you were civill, and knew curtesie,
You would not doe me thus much injury.   L 154 - c

Can you not hate me, as I know you doe,
But you must joyne in soules[1] to mocke me to?

If you are[2] men, as men you are in show,
You would not use a gentle Lady so;
To vow, and sweare, and superpraise my parts,
When I am sure you hate me with your hearts.

You both are Rivals, and love Hermia;
And now both Rivals to mocke Helena.

A trim exploit, a manly enterprize,
To conjure teares up in a poore maids eyes,
With your derision; none of noble sort,
Would so offend a Virgin, and extort
A poore soules patience, all to make you sport.

Lysander   You are unkind Demetrius; be not so,
For you love Hermia; this you know I know;
And here with all good will, with all my heart,
In Hermias love I yeeld you up my part;
And yours of Helena, to me bequeath,
Whom I do love, and will do to[3] my death.

Helena   Never did mockers wast more idle breth.

Demetrius   Lysander, keep thy Hermia, I will none:
If ere I lov'd her, all that love is gone.

My heart to her, but as guest-wise sojourn'd,
And now to Helen it is[4] home return'd,
There to remaine.

Lysander   [5] It is not so.

Demetrius   Disparage not the faith thou dost not know,
Lest to thy perill thou abide[6] it deare.

Looke where thy Love comes, yonder is thy deare.

ENTER HERMIA

L 154 - c / R 154 - c : 3.2.147 - 176

w [1] Qq/Ff = 'soules', modern glosses include 'flouts' 'jeers', 'scoffs', 'scorns'

w [2] F1 = 'are', Qq and most modern texts = 'were'

w [3] F1/Q2 = 'to', Q1 and most modern texts = 'till'

w [4] F1/Q2 = 'it is', Q1 and most modern texts = 'is it'

ADD [5] F1/Q2 show no extra word, Q1 and most modern texts add 'Helen' (which preserves the pentameter)

w [6] F1/Q2 = 'abide', Q1 and most modern texts = 'aby'

Hermia	Dark night, that from the eye his function takes,
	The eare more quicke of apprehension makes,
	Wherein it doth impaire the seeing sense,
	It paies the hearing double recompence.

Thou art not by mine eye, Lysander found,
Mine eare (I thanke it) brought me to that [1] sound.

But why unkindly didst thou leave me so?

Lysander Why should hee stay whom Love doth presse to go[†] ?

Hermia What love could presse Lysander from my side?

Lysander Lysanders love (that would not let him bide)
Faire Helena; who more engilds the night,
Then all yon fierie oes, and eies of light.

Why seek'st thou me?
          Could not this make thee know,
The hate I bare thee, made me leave thee so?

Hermia You speake not as you thinke; it cannot be.

Helena Loe, she is one of this confederacy,
Now I perceive they have conjoyn'd all three,
To fashion this false sport in spight of me.

Injurious Hermia, most ungratefull maid,
Have you conspir'd, have you with these contriv'd
To baite me, with this foule derision?

Is all the counsell that we two have shar'd,
The sisters vowes, the houres that we have spent,
When wee have chid the hasty footed time,
For parting us; O, is all [2] forgot?

All schooledaies friendship, child-hood innocence?

We Hermia, like two Artificiall gods,
Have with our needles, created both one flower,
Both on one sampler, sitting on one cushion,
Both warbling of one song, both in one key;
As if our hands, our sides, voices, and mindes
Had beene incorporate.
          So we grew together,
Like to a double cherry, seeming parted,
But yet a[3] union in partition,

R 154 - c

---

[1] F1 = 'that', Qq and most modern texts = 'thy'

[2] F1/Qq show no extra word, most modern texts add 'quite' (to preserve the pentameter)

[3] F1 = 'a', Qq and most modern texts = 'an'

445
Two lovely berries molded on one stem,
So with two seeming bodies, but one heart,
Two of the first life[1] coats in Heraldry,
Due but to one and crowned with one crest.

And will you rent our ancient love asunder,
450
To joyne with men in scorning your poore friend?

It is not friendly, 'tis not maidenly.

Our sexe as well as I, may chide you for it,
Though I alone doe feele the injurie.

Hermia
I am amazed at your passionate words,
455
I scorne you not; It seemes that you scorne me.

Helena
Have you not set Lysander, as in scorne
To follow me, and praise my eies and face?

And made your other love, Demetrius
(Who even but now did spurne me with his foote)
460
To call me goddesse, nimph, divine, and rare,
Precious, celestiall?
				Wherefore speakes he this
To her he hates?
				And wherefore doth Lysander
465
Denie your love (so rich within his soule)
And tender me (forsooth) affection,
But by your setting on, by your consent?

What though I be not so in grace as you,
So hung upon with love, so fortunate?
470
(But miserable most, to love unlov'd)
This you should pittie, rather then despise.

Hermia
I understand not what you meane by this.

Helena
I, doe, persever, counterfeit sad lookes,
Make mouthes upon me when I turne my backe,
475
Winke each at other, hold the sweete jest up:
This sport well carried, shall be chronicled.

If you have any pittie, grace, or manners,
You would not make me such an argument:
But fare ye well, 'tis partly mine[2] owne fault,
480
Which death or absence soone shall remedie.

Lysander
Stay gentle Helena, heare my excuse,
My love, my life, my soule, faire Helena.

L 155 - d : 3.2.211 - 246

[1] though most modern texts agree with Ff and print 'first life', one interesting gloss = 'first, like'

[2] F1/Q2 = 'mine', Q1 and most modern texts = 'my'

46

Helena	O excellent!	
Hermia	Sweete, do not scorne her so. }	

485   **Demetrius**   If she cannot entreate, I can compell.

Lysander   Thou canst compell, no more then she entreate.
Thy threats have no more strength then her weak praise. [1]
Helen, I love thee, by my life I doe;
I sweare by that which I will lose for thee,
490   To prove him false, that saies I love thee not.

Demetrius   I say, I love thee more then he can do.

Lysander   If thou say so, with-draw and prove it too.

Demetrius   Quick, come.

Hermia   Lysander, whereto tends all this? [2] }

495   **Lysander**   Away, you Ethiope.

Demetrius   No, no, Sir, °[3] seeme to breake loose;
Take on as you would follow, °[4]
But yet come not: you are a tame man, go.

Lysander   Hang off thou cat, thou bur; vile thing let loose,
500   Or I will shake thee from me like a serpent.

Hermia   Why are you growne so rude?
What change is this° sweete Love?

Lysander   Thy love? out tawny Tartar, out;°[5]
Out loathed medicine; O hated poison[6] hence.

505   **Hermia**   Do you not jest?

Helena   Yes sooth, and so do you. }

[W1] F1/Qq = 'praise', most modern texts = 'prayers'

[SD2] most modern texts suggest Hermia contact or confront Lysander physically, hence his next line

[W3] F1/Q2 show no extra words, Q1 and most modern texts = 'heele': some modern texts also follow this with 'but' or 'only', and one interesting gloss changes 'he'll' to 'ye'll'

[LS4] F1 (6/7 or 8 with 'heele'/7 syllables) allows moments for repeated physical action from Hermia which spur on Demetrius' comments, and the resumption of the normal line length suggests when the bulk of the physical action may be over: the modern text two line revision - based in part on Q1 - (9 or 10 with 'heele'/11) blurs the division between language and action, and the moment of resumed 'normalcy'

[LS5] F1's layout (6/6/8 syllables) suggests when Lysander attempts to shake off Hermia: the modern two line rewrite - based in part on Q1 - (10/10) again clouds the precision of the physical action

[W6] F1/Q2 = 'poison', Q1 and most modern texts = 'potion'

47

Lysander	Demetrius: I will keepe my word with thee.	
Demetrius	I would I had your bond: for I perceive A weake bond holds you; Ile not trust your word.	
510 **Lysander**	What, should I hurt her, strike her, kill her dead? Although I hate her, Ile not harme her so.	
Hermia	What, can you do me greater harme then hate? [1]	L 155 - d

Hate me, wherefore?

               O me, what newes my Love?

515   Am not I Hermia?

                       Are not you Lysander?

               I am as faire now, as I was ere while.

               Since night you lov'd me; [†2] yet since night you left me.

               Why then you left me (O the gods forbid[3]

520   In earnest, shall I say?

                         }

Lysander	I, by my life; And never did desire to see thee more.	

               Therefore be out of hope, of question, of[4] doubt;

               Be certaine, nothing truer: 'tis no jest,

525   That I doe hate thee, and love Helena.

Hermia	O me, you jugler, you canker blossome, You theefe of love; What, have you come by night, And stolne my loves heart from him?	

                         }

Helena	Fine yfaith:	

530   Have you no modesty, no maiden shame,

               No touch of bashfulnesse?

                                What, will you teare

               Impatient answers from my gentle tongue?

               Fie, fie, you counterfeit, you puppet, you.

535   **Hermia**   Puppet? why so?

                       I, that way goes the game.

               Now I perceive that she hath made compare

               Betweene our statures, she hath urg'd her height,

---

L 155 - d / R 155 - d : 3.2.266 - 291

[SD 1] one contemporary director suggests Hermia now releases Lysander

[W 2] F1 = 'lov'dme', F2/Qq/most modern texts = 'lov'd me'

[PCT 3] Qq/F2/most modern texts close the parenthesis here, F1 sets the sentence with the bracket incomplete

[W 4] F1/Qq = 'of', most modern texts omit the word (thus maintaining a ten syllable line)

	And with her personage, her tall personage,
40	Her height (forsooth) she hath prevail'd with him.
	And are you growne so high in his esteeme,
	Because I am so dwarfish, and so low?
	How low am I, thou painted May-pole?
	Speake,
45	How low am I?
	I am not yet so low,
	But that my nailes can reach unto thine eyes. [1]
Helena	I pray you though you mocke me, gentlemen,
	Let her not hurt me; I was never curst:
50	I have no gift at all in shrewishnesse;
	I am a right maide for my cowardize;
	Let her not strike me: you perhaps may thinke,
	Because she is something lower then my selfe,
	That I can match her.
55	**Hermia**	Lower? harke againe.
Helena	Good Hermia, do not be so bitter with me,
	I evermore did love you Hermia,
	Did ever keepe your counsels, never wronged you,
	Save that in love unto Demetrius,
60	I told him of your stealth unto this wood.
	He followed you, for love I followed him,
	But he hath chid me hence, and threatned me
	To strike me, spurne me, nay to kill me too;
	And now, so you will let me quiet go,
65	To Athens will I beare my folly backe,
	And follow you no further.
	Let me go.
	You see how simple, and how fond I am.
Hermia	Why get you gone: who ist that hinders you?
570 **Helena**	A foolish heart that I leave here behinde.
Hermia	What, with Lysander?
{Helena} [2]	With Demetrius.
Lysander	Be not afraid, she shall not harme thee Helena. [3]

R 155 - d : 3.2.292 - 321

[SD][1] most modern texts suggest Hermia now lunges at Helena

[P][2] F1 assigns this to Hermia (which makes no theatrical sense), F3/Qq/most modern texts give it to Helena

[SD][3] most modern texts indicate that the two men move in to protect Helena

Demetrius	No sir, she shall not, though you take her part.
Helena	O when she's¹ angry, she is keene and shrewd,
	She was a vixen when she went to schoole,
	And though she be but little, she is fierce.
Hermia	Little againe?
	Nothing but low and little?
	Why will you suffer her to flout me thus?
	Let me come to her.
Lysander	Get you gone you dwarfe,
	You minimus, of hindring knot-grasse made,
	You bead, you acorne.
Demetrius	You are too officious,
	In her behalfe that scornes your services.
	Let her alone, speake not of Helena,
	Take not her part.
	For if thou dost intend
	Never so little shew of love to her,
	Thou shalt abide it.
Lysander	Now she holds me not,
	Now follow if thou dar'st, to try whose right,
	Of thine or mine is most in Helena.
Demetrius	Follow?
	Nay, Ile goe with thee cheeke by
	jowle.

R 155 - d

[Exit Lysander and Demetrius]

Hermia	You Mistris, all this coyle is long of you. ²
	Nay, goe not backe.
Helena	I will not trust you I,
	Nor longer stay in your curst companie.
	Your hands then mine, are quicker for a fray,
	My legs are longer though to runne away. ³

∞⁴

R 155 - d / L 156 - d : 3.2.322 - 344

W ¹ F1/Q2 = 'she's', Q1 and most modern texts = 'she is'

SD ² most modern texts indicate Helena begins to move away

SD ³ most modern texts add a stage direction here for Helena to exit at top speed

ADD/SD ⁴ F1 omits a line printed in Qq and all modern texts, viz.

      Hermia   I am amaz'd, and know not what to say.

most modern texts add the direction for Hermia's exit - though Q's direction [exeunt] suggests a group exit

ENTER OBERON AND PUCKE [1]

Oberon	This is thy negligence, still thou mistak'st,
	Or else committ'st thy knaveries willingly. [2]
Pucke [3]	Beleeve me, King of shadowes, I mistooke,
	Did not you tell me, I should know the man,
	By the Athenian garments he hath[4] on?
	And so farre blamelesse proves my enterpize,
	That I have nointed an Athenians eies,
	And so farre am I glad, it so did sort,
	As this their jangling I esteeme a sport.
Oberon	Thou seest these Lovers seeke a place to fight,
	Hie therefore Robin, overcast the night,
	The starrie Welkin cover thou anon,
	With drooping fogge as blacke as Acheron,
	And lead these testie Rivals so astray,
	As one come not within anothers way.
	Like to Lysander, sometime frame thy tongue,
	Then stirre Demetrius up with bitter wrong;
	And sometime raile thou like Demetrius;
	And from each other looke thou leade them thus,
	Till ore their browes, death-counterfeiting, sleepe
	With leaden legs, and Battie-wings doth creepe; [†5]
	Then crush this hearbe into Lysanders eie, [6]
	Whose liquor hath this vertuous propertie,
	To take from thence all error, with his might,
	And make his eie-bals role with wonted sight.
	When they next wake, all this derision
	Shall seeme a dreame, and fruitlesse vision,
	And backe to Athens shall the Lovers wend
	With league, whose date till death shall never end.
	Whiles I in this affaire do thee imply, [7]
	Ile to my Queene, and beg her Indian Boy;

[SD 1] since Oberon and Pucke/Robin have been on-stage throughout the lovers' quarrel, most modern texts alter the direction to suggest they simply come forward

[W 2] F1 = 'willingly', Qq and most modern texts = 'wilfully'

[P 3] this is the first time the character directly blames Oberon for the mistakes, and it's interesting to note that the character keeps the guise of Pucke to do so

[W 4] F1 = 'hath', Qq and most modern texts = 'had'

[W 5] F1 = 'c reepe', F2/Qq/most modern texts = 'creepe'

[SD 6] most modern texts indicate that Oberon gives Pucke the herb ♭

[W 7] Q1 = 'imploy', Q2 = 'apply', F1 = 'imply', most modern texts = 'employ'

35 And then I will her charmed eie release
From monsters view, and all things shall be peace.

Pucke My Fairie Lord, this must be done with haste,
For night-swift [1] Dragons cut the Clouds full fast,
And yonder shines Auroras harbinger;
40 At whose approach Ghosts wandring here and there,
Troope home to Church-yards; damned spirits all,
That in crosse-waies and flouds have buriall,
Alreadie to their wormie beds are gone;
For feare least day should looke their shames upon,
45 [2] They wilfully themselves exile[†3] from light,
And must for aye consort with blacke browd night.

Oberon But we are spirits of another sort:
I, with the mornings love have oft made sport,
And like a Forrester, the groves may tread,
50 Even till the Easterne gate all fierie red,
Opening on Neptune, with faire blessed beames,
Turnes into yellow gold, his salt greene streames.   L 156 - d

But notwithstanding haste, make no delay:
We may effect this businesse, yet ere day. [4]

55 **Pucke** Up and downe, up and downe, ° **I will leade**
them up and downe/ : ° I am fear'd in field and towne . °
Goblin, lead them up and downe :/° here comes one . [5]

ENTER LYSANDER [6]

L 156 - d / R 156 - d : 3.2.376 - 400

[W] [1] F1/Q2 = 'night-swift', Q1 and most modern texts = 'nights swift'

[LS] [2] at least one modern text suggests these two lines should start Oberon's speech

[W] [3] F1 = 'dxile', Qq/F2 = 'exile', most modern texts = 'exil'd'

[SD] [4] most modern texts add a stage direction here for Oberon to exit

[LS] [5] Q1 prints the spell as two long lines plus a short one as the first 'victim' arrives - as shown by the symbol
/: after the first six words the pattern is written in the reversed iambic/heartbeat of magic and ritual - but in a
much longer line (13/14 syllables); accordingly, most modern texts split the two long lines into four, as
shown by the symbol °: F1 layout was probably created because of lack of space at the top of the
column to allow for all the text that had to be set: if the reader accepts that F1 is improperly set Q1 verse,
then it can be seen that Pucke/Robin has difficulty in creating and/or sustaining the first line of the required
magic

[SD.LS] [6] the following sequence is based on the premise that Robin/Pucke is invisible, that he can mimic
both Lysander's and Demetrius' voices, and that he keeps moving all over the stage, and on and off stage,
to confuse the would-be combatants: many modern texts add a confusing multitude of stage directions to
explain each moment instead of leaving the action to the actors' and readers' imaginations; they also turn
some of the broken text into regular poetry, thus blurring over moments for the characters where the play
demands they should be in danger of losing control

Lysander		Where art thou, proud Demetrius? → [1]
		Speake thou now.
660	**·Robin·** [2]	Here villaine, drawne & readie.
		Where art thou?

Lysander	I will be with thee straight.
Robin	Follow me then° to plainer ground.
	ENTER DEMETRIUS
Demetrius	Lysander, speake againe; °[3]

665		Thou runaway, thou coward, art thou[†4] fled?
		Speake[5] in some bush: Where dost thou[†] hide thy head?
	Robin	Thou coward, art thou bragging to the stars,
		Telling the bushes that thou look'st for wars,
		And wilt not come?
670		Come recreant, come thou childe,
		Ile whip thee with a rod.
		He is defil'd
		That drawes a sword on thee.
		}
	Demetrius	Yea, art thou there?
675	**Robin**	Follow my voice, we'l try no manhood here.
		[Exit] [6]
	Lysander	He goes before me, and still dares me on,
		When I come where he cals, then he's[7] gone.
		The villaine is much lighter heel'd then I:
		I followed fast, but faster he did flye;

[LS1] F1's tiny break offers both Robin and Lysander a moment of physicality (thus setting up expectations for the rest of the scene): most modern texts follow (the non-acting script) Q1 and print this as one line

[P2] notice that it was Pucke who created the spell, but Robin who has the fun of deceiving them

[LS3] modern restructuring (two regular lines, 10/10 syllables) regularises the physical potential of F1/Qq's 6/8/6, which cover Robin/Pucke's need to get Lysander away from the about-to-enter furious Demetrius, as well as the exit, (which most modern texts add as a stage direction) and entry

[W4] F1 sets 'tho u' here and 'th ou' in the next line: F2/most modern texts = 'thou' both times

[PCT5] F1/Qq show no punctuation; some modern texts punctuate to 'Speak! In some bush:'

[SD6] most modern texts add a stage direction for Lysander's entry, and The Oxford Complete Works, both editions, op. cit., suggests that a new scene should start here, the idea being that it is in a deeper part of the wood ('the higher ground') and that the would-be combatants are much more tired (and disheveled?)

[W7] F1/Q2 = 'he's', Q1 and most modern texts = 'he is' (which maintains the pentameter)

[shifting places] [1]

That fallen am I in darke uneven way,
And here wil rest me.
Come thou gentle day:

[lye down]

For if but once thou shew me thy gray light,
Ile finde Demetrius, and revenge this spight. [2]

ENTER ROBIN AND DEMETRIUS

Robin	Ho, ho, ho; coward, why com'st thou not?
Demetrius	Abide me, if thou dar'st. For well I wot, Thou runst before me, shifting every place, And dar'st not stand, nor looke me in the face. Where art thou ? [3]
Robin	Come hither, I am here. }
Demetrius	Nay then thou mock'st me; thou shalt buy this deere, If ever I thy face by day-light see.
	Now goe thy way: faintnesse constraineth me, To measure out my length on this cold bed, [4] By daies approach looke to be visited. [5]

ENTER HELENA

Helena	O weary night, O long and tedious night, Abate thy houres, shine comforts from the East, That I may backe to Athens by day-light, From these that my poore companie detest; And sleepe that sometime [6] shuts up sorrowes eie, Steale me a while from mine owne companie.

R 156 - d : 3.2.417 - 436

[SD 1] this stage direction seems to cause many modern editors great difficulty, see The Oxford Companion, op. cit., page 283, footnote re 3.2.405/1384: however, the difficulty arises because they assume it refers to Robin/Pucke: in the F1 placing it can only apply to Lysander, and as such is perfectly understandable

[SD 2] most modern texts add a stage direction that Lysander falls asleep

[W 3] F1/Q2 show no extra word, Q1 and most modern texts = 'now' (which maintains a ten syllable line)

[SD 4] most modern texts suggest Demetrius now lies down (though he could have done so on the previous line)

[SD 5] most modern texts add a stage direction here that Demetrius falls asleep

[W 6] F1/Q2 = 'sometime', Q1 and most modern texts = 'sometimes'

[Sleepe]

Robin	Yet but three ?	

5 Come one more,[1]
Two of both kindes makes up foure .

Here she comes, curst and sad,
Cupid is a knavish lad,

ENTER HERMIA [2]

Thus to make poore females mad .

0 **Hermia** Never so wearie, never so in woe,
Bedabbled with the dew, and torne with briars,
I can no further crawle, no further goe ;
My legs can keepe no pace with my desires .

Here will I rest me till the breake of day,
5 Heavens shield Lysander, if they meane a fray. [3]

Robin On the ground ° sleepe sound, °
Ile apply° [4] your eie° gentle lover, remedy. °

[5] **When thou wak'st** , ° **thou tak'st** ° [6]
True delight° in the sight° of thy former Ladies eye, °   R156 - d

---

R 156 - d : 3.2.437 - 457

M [1]
as when Robin/Pucke began the magic to darken the sky, so here the first line of the ritual is difficult for him to sustain as a completely reversed heartbeat - although linguistically the slight pause between the two phrases can be counted as a moment of breath release, and thus poetically as a silent weak (unstressed) beat: this breaking or inability to sustain for more than a line or two becomes a predominant feature for the remainder of Robin/Pucke's action in the scene (perhaps he is exhausted from all the running around he has had to do, perhaps four people are too many for him to cope with, perhaps he is distracted by the women, perhaps he is truly scared by the approaching dawn, or perhaps - as has happened repeatedly throughout the play - he is unable to complete anything properly as bidden)

SD [2]
Qq do not set an entry for Hermia, and some modern texts advance Ff's entry by at least two lines (just before Pucke's 'Here she comes....'): however, the Ff setting allows Pucke and the audience to hear her (crashing through the undergrowth?) before she finally appears

SD [3]
most modern texts add a stage direction that Hermia lies down and falls asleep

ADD [4]
F1/Qq print no extra word, most modern texts = 'to'

MLS [5]
the F1/Qq layout for the following magic spell is wonderfully erratic, and though in F1 it is set over a page split and thus white space might have accounted for the layout, F1 and Q1 are set identically save for the last word and Q1 sets its text in the middle of a column: modern texts have relineated as shown, making the highly irregular appear as regularised doggerel: however, the source text identifies the character as Robin when attempting to undo the mistakes he was partially responsible for as Pucke - though earlier in the play all his magic was undertaken as Pucke and now, as the italics suggest, he is only capable of uttering the purely magic lines three times: either the F1/Qq text stands as is and he is unsure and/or incapable of finishing the job successfully (see footnote #1 above), or, through the modern restructurings and occasional momentary breath pauses, he neatly ties up all the loose ends

SD [6]
most modern texts add a stage direction that Robin/Pucke now applies the love-juice to Lysander's eye: this is a rather dreadful assumption on two counts; first, they do not suggest that Demetrius should be similarly released - and thus the implication is that his rediscovered love for Helena is based only on magical intervention (see footnote #5, Act Two Scene 1, this script page 20); second, it suggests that Robin/Pucke is in full control of what he is doing, something the metre of the lines flatly deny

20   **And the Country Proverb knowne,**
      That every man should take his owne,
      In your waking shall be showne .

      Jacke shall have Jill,° nought shall goe ill,°
      The man shall have his Mare againe, and all shall bee
25   well .

THEY SLEEPE ALL THE ACT

Actus Quartus [1]

ENTER QUEENE OF FAIRIES, AND CLOWNE,[2] AND FAIRIES, AND THE KING BEHINDE THEM [3]

Titania	Come, sit thee downe upon this flowry bed,
	While I thy amiable cheekes doe coy,
	And sticke muske roses in thy sleeke smoothe head,
	And kisse thy faire large eares, my gentle joy.

5 **Clowne**
Bottome as
Where's Pease blossome?

Pease-blossome Ready.

Clowne Scratch my head, Pease-blossome.
Wher's Moun-
sieuer[4] Cobweb.

10 **Cobweb** Ready.

Clowne Mounsieur Cobweb, good Mounsier get [5] your
weapons in your hand, & kill me a red hipt humble-Bee,
on the top of a thistle; and good Mounsieur bring mee
the hony bag.
15 Doe not fret your selfe too much in the
action, Mounsieur; and good Mounsieur have a care the
hony bag breake not, I would be loth to have you[†6] over-
flowne with a hony-bag signiour. [7]
Where's Mounsieur
20 Mustardseed?

L 157 - c : 4.1.1 - 17

[ALT 1] stemming from its suggestion of a new scene on page 53, footnote #5, The Oxford Complete Works, op. cit., suggests that this should not be considered a new act but flow on from the previous scene

[P 2] Bottome's prefix has been altered to Piramus before, but this is the first time since his transformation that F1/Qq refer to him as Clowne, which could be a wonderful signal that he may now be behaving in a style the reader/audience has not seen before: certainly, as he becomes accustomed to the blandishments and trappings of Fairyland so his requests and language become more familiar and rustic

[SD 3] some modern texts omit Oberon in this entry, bringing him on with Robin/Pucke (see footnote #3, page 59)

[W 4] Bottome repeats the French title he gives Cobweb three times in succession, and F1 spells it three different ways, 'Mounsieuer', 'Mounsieur' and 'Mounsier', perhaps suggesting he is having fun with the word: however all other Ff/Qq/modern texts standardise the spelling

[W 5] F1/Q2 show no word here, Q1 and most modern texts = 'you'

[W 6] F1 = 'yon', Qq/F2/most modern texts = 'you'

[SD 7] most modern texts add a stage direction for Cobweb to exit

Mustardseed	Ready.
Clowne	Give me your neafe, Mounsieur Mustardseed. Pray you leave your courtesie good Mounsieur.
Mustardseed	What's your will?
25 **Clowne**	Nothing good Mounsieur, but to help Cavalery Cobweb[1] to scratch. I must to the Barbers Mounsieur, for me-thinkes I am marvellous hairy about the face. And I
30	am such a tender asse, if my haire do but tickle me, I must scratch.
Titania	What, wilt thou heare some musicke, my sweet love.
Clowne	I have a reasonable good eare in musicke. Let
35	us[2] have the tongs and the bones.

MUSICKE TONGS, RURALL MUSICKE

Titania	Or say sweete Love, what thou desirest to eat.
Clowne	Truly a pecke of Provender; I could munch your good dry Oates. Me-thinkes I have a great desire to a bottle of hay: good hay, sweete hay hath no fel-low.

Titania	I have a venturous Fairy, That shall seeke the Squirrels hoard/, And fetch thee new Nuts.° [3]

45	
Clowne	I had rather have a handfull or two of dried pease. ° But I pray you let none of your people stirre me, ° I have an exposition of sleepe come upon me. ° [4]

L 157 · c : 4.1.18 - 39

P 1   either Cobweb did not exit to find the honey as ordered earlier, or it is Pease-blossome who is doing the scratching, as requested: F1/Qq = 'Cobweb', some modern texts = 'Pease-blossome'

W 2   F1/Q2 = 'let us', Q1 and most modern texts = 'Let's'

LS 3   the broken layout of F1 (especially as modified from Q1, shown by the symbol /) allows for splendid momentary gaps as Titania waxes enthusiastic and (perhaps) the Fairies hide or volunteer

VP 4   though Bottome never speaks verse as himself or under the prefix Clowne, some modern texts print this one speech in verse as the symbol ° shows

50	**Titania**	Sleepe thou, and I will winde thee in my arms,
		Fairies be gone, and be alwaies away. [1]
		So doth the woodbine, the sweet Honisuckle,
		Gently entwist; the female Ivy so
		Enrings the barky fingers of the Elme.
55		O how I love thee! how I dote on thee! [2]

L 157 - c

ENTER ROBIN GOODFELLOW AND OBERON [3]

	Oberon	Welcome good Robin: → [4]
		Seest thou this sweet sight?
		Her dotage now I doe begin to pitty.
		For meeting her of late behinde the wood,
60		Seeking sweet savors[5] for this hatefull foole,
		I did upbraid her, and fall out with her.
		For she his hairy temples then had rounded,
		With coronet of fresh and fragrant flowers.
		And that same dew which somtime on the buds,
65		Was wont to swell like round and orient pearles;
		Stood now within the pretty flouriets[6] eyes,
		Like teares that did their owne disgrace bewaile.
		When I had at my pleasure taunted her,
		And she in milde termes beg'd my patience,
70		I then did aske of her, her changeling childe,
		Which straight she gave me, and her Fairy sent
		To beare him to my Bower in Fairy Land.
		And now I have the Boy, I will undoe
		This hatefull imperfection of her eyes.
75		And gentle Pucke, take this transformed scalpe,
		From off the head of this Athenian swaine;
		That he awaking when the other doe,
		May all to Athens backe againe repaire,
		And thinke no more of this nights accidents,
80		But as the fierce vexation of a dreame.

L 157 - c / R 157 - c : 4.1.40 - 69

[SD 1] most modern texts add a stage direction for the exit of the Fairies

[SD 2] most modern texts suggest they fall asleep entwined

[SD 3] Q1/some modern texts just bring in Robin, suggesting since Oberon was already on-stage he now advances: others ignore F1's opening Act Four stage direction and now bring in Oberon for the first time in the scene

[SP 4] Q1 prints this as one line as do most editions (suggesting white space prevented F1 from so doing): however, F1's reading does allow Oberon a brief personal silent moment before continuing

[W 5] F1/Q2 = 'savors', Q1 and most modern texts = 'favours'

[W 6] F1/Qq = 'flouriets', most modern texts = 'flourets'

	But first I will release the Fairy Queene.
	[1] [2] **Be thou[3] as thou wast wont to be ;**
	See as thou wast wont to see .
	Dians bud, or[4] Cupids flower,
	Hath such force and blessed power .
	Now my Titania wake you my sweet Queene.
Titania [5]	My Oberon, what visions have I seene!
	Me-thought I was enamoured of an Asse.
Oberon	There lies your love .
Titania	How came these things to passe?
	Oh, how mine eyes doth[6] loath this[7] visage now!
Oberon	Silence a while.
	Robin take off his[8] head :
	Titania, musick call, and strike more dead
	Then common sleepe; of all these, fine[9] the sense.
Titania	Musicke, ho[10] musicke, such as charmeth sleepe.

[Musick still]

Robin	[11] **When thou wak'st, with thine owne fooles eies**
	peepe.
Oberon	Sound musick; [12] come my Queen, take hands with me†
	And rocke the ground whereon these sleepers be. [13]

R 157 - c : 4.1.70 - 86

[M][1] possibly this could be sung, since throughout the rest of Ff text this is the only magic (save the songs themselves) set in italics, the font normally reserved for - amongst other things - poems, letters or song

[SD][2] most modern texts suggest Oberon pours the love juice into Titania's eye: however, if 'o'er' is substituted for 'or' (see footnote #4 below) then he would use something reflecting Diana, the goddess of both the hunt and chastity i.e. what he refers to in two lines time as 'Dian's bud'

[W/M][3] F1 = 'thou', Qq and most modern texts do not print the word (without it the magic pattern is maintained)

[W][4] F1/Qq = 'or' (as in 'either/or'), most modern texts = 'o'er' (meaning 'over')

[SD][5] most modern texts explain Titania now awakes

[W][6] F1/Q2 = 'doth', Q1 and most modern texts = 'doe'

[W][7] F1/Q2 = 'this', Q1 and most modern texts = 'his'

[W][8] Qq/most modern texts = 'this', Ff = 'his'

[W/PCT][9] F1/Qq = comma followed by 'fine', some modern texts = no punctuation followed by 'five'

[W][10] F1/Q2 and most modern texts = 'ho', Q1 and some modern texts = 'how'

[SD][11] most modern texts add Robin/Pucke removes the ass's head from Bottome (note he uses magic to do so)

[SD][12] most modern texts suggest that now the style of the music changes

[SD][13] most modern texts add a stage direction that here Oberon and Titania dance to the new music (perhaps with their Fairies - whom some texts allow to creep back in at some point during the reconciliation)

Now thou and I are new in amity,
And will to morrow midnight, solemnly
Dance in Duke Theseus house triumphantly,
And blesse it to all faire posterity. [1]

05   There shall the paires of faithfull Lovers be
Wedded, with Theseus, all in jollity.

Robin   [2]   **Faire** [3] **King , attend, and marke,**
I doe heare the morning Larke.

Obcron   **Then my Queene in silence sad,**
10   **Trip we after the** [4] **nights shade ;**
We the Globe can compasse soone,
Swifter then the wandring Moone .

Titania   **Come my Lord, and in our flight,**
Tell me how it came this night,
15   **That I sleeping heere was found,**

[Sleepers Lye still] [5]   R 157 - c

With these mortals on the ground .

[Exeunt]
WINDE HORNES
ENTER THESEUS, EGEUS, HIPPOLITA AND ALL HIS TRAINE

Theseus   Goe one of you, finde out the Forrester,
For now our observation is perform'd;
And since we have the vaward of the day,
20   My Love shall heare the musicke of my hounds.

Uncouple in the Westerne valley, let them goe ;
Dispatch I say, and finde the Forrester. [6]

We will faire Queene, up to the Mountaines top,[7]

R 157 - c / L 158 - c :   4.1.87 - 109

W [1] F1/Q2 = 'posterity', Q1 and most modern texts = 'prosperitie'

M [2] even though the character is still termed Robin, it is he who starts the ritual speech pattern, and it seems to require the powers of all three Fairies to perform the magical ritual which allows them to leave unharmed by the rapidly approaching dawn

W [3] Ff = 'Faire', Qq and most modern texts = 'Fairy' (which would allow for a full line of magic)

WM [4] F1/Q2 = 'the', Q1 and most modern texts omit the word, almost preserving the pattern of magical speech

SD [5] F1/2 print this direction at the bottom of R157 instead of at the end of the speech: Qq set no direction: most modern texts place it with the entry, suggesting the sleepers are lying away from the new action

SD [6] most modern texts add a stage direction for one of his 'Traine' to exit

PCT [7] F1's punctuation is unclear, F2/Qq/most modern texts set a comma

25		And marke the musicall confusion Of[†1] hounds and eccho in conjunction.
	Hippolita	I was with Hercules and Cadmus once, When in a wood of Creete they bayed the Beare With hounds of Sparta; never did I heare Such gallant chiding.
30		For besides the groves, The skies, the fountaines, every region neere, Seeme[2] all one mutuall cry.
		I never heard So musicall a discord, such sweet thunder.
35	**Theseus**	My hounds are bred out of the Spartan kinde, So flew'd, so sanded, and their heads are hung With eares that sweepe away the morning dew, Crooke kneed, and dew-lapt, like Thessalian Buls, Slow in pursuit, but match'd in mouth like bels,
40		Each under each.
		A cry more tuneable Was never hallowed[3] to, nor cheer'd with horne, In Creete, in Sparta, nor in Thessaly; Judge when you heare.
45		But soft, what nimphs are these?
	Egeus	My Lord, this is my daughter heere asleepe, And this Lysander, this Demetrius is, This Helena, olde Nedars Helena, I wonder of this[4] being heere together.
50	**Theseus**	No doubt they rose up early, to observe The right[5] of May; and hearing our intent, Came heere in grace of our solemnity.
		But speake Egeus, is not this the day That Hermia should give answer of her choice?
155	**Egeus**	It is, my Lord.
	Theseus	Goe bid the hunts-men wake them with their hornes.

L 158 - c : 4.1.110 - 138

W [1] F1 = 'Ofhounds', F2/Qq/most modern texts = 'Of hounds'

W [2] F1/Qq = 'Seeme', F2 and most modern texts = 'Seem'd'

W [3] Q1 = 'hollowed', F1 = 'hallowed', most modern texts = 'holla'd'

W [4] F1/Q2 = 'this', Q1 and most modern texts = 'their'

W [5] F1/Qq = 'right', most modern texts = 'rite' (thus removing the rather pointed pun/wordplay of Theseus)

¹ **HORNES AND THEY WAKE
SHOUT WITHIN, THEY ALL START UP**

Theseus	Good morrow friends: Saint Valentine is past,
	Begin these wood birds but to couple now?
Lysander	Pardon my Lord. ²
Theseus	I pray you all stand up.
	I know you two are Rivall enemies.
	How comes this gentle concord in the world,
	That hatred is is so farre from jealousie,
	To sleepe by hate, and feare no enmity.
Lysander	My Lord, I shall reply amazedly,
	Halfe sleepe, halfe waking.
	But as yet, I sweare,
	I cannot truly say how I came heere.
	But as I thinke (for truly would I speake)
	And now I doe bethinke me, so it is;
	I came with Hermia hither.
	Our intent
	Was to be gone from Athens, where we might be³
	Without the perill of the Athenian Law. ⁴
Egeus	Enough, enough, my Lord: you have enough;
	I beg^{† 5} the Law, the Law, upon his head:
	They would have stolne away, they would Demetrius,
	Thereby to have defeated you and me:
	You of your wife, and me of my consent;
	Of my consent, that she should be your wife.
Demetrius	My Lord, faire Helen told me of their stealth,
	Of this their purpose hither, to this wood,
	And I in furie hither followed them;
	Faire Helena, in fancy followed ⁶ me.

Line numbers (left margin): 60, 65, 70, 75, 80, 85 (shown as ·60, ·65, ·70, ·75, ·80, 185)

L 158 - c

L 158 - c / R 158 - c : 4.139 - 163

^{SD}₁ some modern texts add to the stage direction for someone to exit to signal the huntsmen

^{SD}₂ to justify Theseus' next line, some modern texts add a stage direction here that they kneel: (however, the 'start up' in the previous direction does not necessarily mean the exhausted lovers are already on their feet; it could just be that from their initial sleepy awaking - the first direction - they are shocked/ startled into full consciousness - the second direction - when they realise where they are and with whom)

^W₃ F1/Q2 = 'be', Q1 and most modern texts omit the word

^{PCT}₄ F1/Q2 = a period; Q1 = a comma and most modern texts = a dash (as if Egeus interrupts him)

^W₅ F1 = 'b eg', F2/Qq/most modern texts = 'beg'

^W₆ F1/Q2 = 'followed', Q1 and most modern texts = 'following'

But my good Lord, I wot not by what power,

> (But by some power it is) my love
> To Hermia° (melted as the snow)
> Seemes to me now° as the remembrance of an idle gaude,° 1

90   Which in my childehood I did doat upon:
And all the faith, the vertue of my heart,
The object and the pleasure of mine eye,
Is onely Helena.
                        To her, my Lord,
95   Was I betroth'd, ere I see² Hermia,
But likc a sickcnesse did I loath this food,
But as in health, come to my naturall taste,
Now doe I³ wish it, love it, long for it,
And will for evermore be true to it.

00   **Theseus**   Faire Lovers, you are fortunately met;
Of this discourse we shall heare more anon. 4

Egeus, I will over-beare your will;
For in the Temple, by and by with us,
These couples shall eternally be knit.

205   And for the morning now is something worne,
Our purpos'd hunting shall be set aside.

Away, with us to Athens; three and three,
Wee'll hold a feast in great solemnitie.

Come Hippolita.

[Exit Duke and Lords] 5

210   **Demetrius**   These things seeme small & undistinguishable,
Like farre off mountaines turned into Clouds.

Hermia   Me-thinks I see these things with parted eye,
When every things⁶ seemes double.
                                                          }

LS 1 the F1/Qq lineation is wonderfully revealing: following an emotional (though highly ungrammatical)
period, the two slightly short lines (8 or 9/8 or 9 syllables) give Demetrius two halting attempts to explain
before rushing into a fourteen syllable admission: the modern restructuring (11 - 13/9/10) totally destroys
the psychology of the build from hesitancy to explosion that was originally given him

W 2 F1/Q1 = 'see', Q2 and most modern texts = 'saw'

W 3 F1/Q2 = 'doe I', Q1 and most modern texts = 'I doe'

W 4 F1= 'we shall heare more anon', Q2 = 'we will heare more anon', Q1 and most modern texts = 'we more
will here anon'

SD 5 most modern texts add Hippolita to the exit

W 6 F1 = 'things', Qq/F3/most modern texts = 'thing'

Helena		So me-thinkes:
5		And I have found Demetrius, like a jewell,
		Mine owne, and not mine owne.

)

Demetrius	[1]	It seemes to mee,
		That yet we sleepe, we dreame.

                                        Do not you thinke,

20   The Duke was heere, and bid us follow him?

Hermia	Yea, and my Father.

)

Helena	And Hippolita.

Lysander	And he [2] bid us follow to the Temple.

Demetrius	Why then we are awake; lets follow him,° and
25	by the way let us recount our dreames. [3]

BOTTOME WAKES
[Exit Lovers] [4]

Clowne	When my cue comes, call me, and I will answer.
	My next is, most faire Piramus.

                                  Hey ho Peter Quince?

Flute the bellowes-mender?

30   Snout the tinker?

                                    Starve-

ling?

      Gods my life!

                       Stolne hence, and left me asleepe: I

35   have had a most rare vision.

                           I [5] had a dreame, past the wit

of man, to say, what dreame it was.

                         Man is but an Asse,

if he goe about to expound this dreame.

40   Me-thought I

was, there is no man can tell what.

R 158 - c : 4.1.190 - 208

ADD [1] F1 omits two half lines given to Demetrius at the opening of this speech in Qq (and printed in most modern texts), viz. 'Are you sure/That we are awake?'

W [2] F1 and some modern texts set no extra word, Qq and some modern texts print 'did'

VP [3] though F1/Qq all print the ending of the scene as a tail-off into prose as the four lovers leave the magic of the wood, sadly many modern texts regularise the two lines back into verse as the symbol ° shows

SD [4] it's a great shame that most modern texts reverse this stage direction, allowing the Lovers to exit before Bottome awakes, for the idea of them being chased out by his grunts and snuffles is quite lovely

W [5] F1 shows no extra word, Qq and most modern texts = 'have'

                        Me-thought I was,
and me-thought I had.
                        But man is but a patch'd foole,
if he will offer to say, what me-thought I had.
                        The eye of
man hath not heard, the eare of man hath not seen, mans
hand is not able to taste, his tongue to conceive, nor his
heart to report, what my dreame was.
                        I will get Peter
Quince to write a ballet [1] of this dreame, it shall be called
Bottomes Dreame, because it hath no bottome; and I will
sing it in the latter end of a play, before the Duke.
                        Per-
adventure, to make it the more gracious, I shall sing it
at her death.

[Exit]
ENTER QUINCE, FLUTE, THISBIE, [2] SNOUT, AND STARVELING
[Most modern texts create a new scene here, Act Four, Scene 2]

·Quince·	Have you sent to Bottomes house? Is he come home yet?
Starveling	He cannot be heard of. Out of doubt hee is transported. R 158 - c
Thisbie	If he come not, then the play is mar'd. It goes not forward, doth it?
Quince	It is not possible: you have not a man in all Athens, able to discharge Piramus but he.
Thisbie	No, hee hath simply the best wit of any handy- craft man in Athens.
Quince	Yea, and the best person too, and hee is a very Paramour, for a sweet voyce.

R 158 - c / L 159 - c : 4.1.208 - 4.2.12

W [1] F1/Qq = 'ballet', F4 and some modern texts = 'ballad'
SD [2] F1/Qq suggest both Flute and 'Thisbie' come on-stage, which is impossible: however, Flute could be
  bringing on Thisbie's costume which he could endow with a life of its own; after all though not
  performing as the character, the F1/Qq prefix refers to him constantly as 'This.' whereas the prefixes for the
  rest of the Mechanicals are their real names: also, the Q1 stage direction refers to Starveling and Snout
  rather uncharitably as the Rabble

| Thisbie | You must say, Paragon. |
| | A Paramour is (God blesse us) a thing of nought. [1] |

ENTER SNUG THE JOYNER

| Snug | Masters, the Duke is comming from the Temple, and there is two or three Lords & Ladies more married. |
| | If our sport had gone forward, we had all bin made men. |

Thisbie	O sweet bully Bottome: thus hath he lost sixepence a day, during his life; he could not have scaped sixpence a day.
	And the Duke had not given him sixpence a day for playing Piramus, Ile be hang'd.
	He would have deserved it.
	Sixpence a day in Piramus, or nothing.

ENTER BOTTOME

| ˙Bottome˙ | Where are these Lads? |
| | Where are these hearts? |

| Quince | Bottome, ô most couragious day! |
| | O most happie houre! |

Bottome	Masters, I am to discourse wonders; but ask me not what.
	For if I tell you, I am no[2] true Athenian.
	I will tell you every thing [3] as it fell out.

| Quince | Let us heare, sweet Bottome. |

| Bottome | Not a word of me: all that I will tell you, is, that the Duke hath dined. |
| | Get your apparell together, good strings to your beards, new ribbands to your pumps, meete presently at the Palace, every man looke ore his part: for the short and the long is, our play is preferred: |

L 159 - c : 4.2.13 - 39

W [1] F1/Qq = 'nought', most modern texts follow F2 = 'naught'

W [2] F1 = 'no', Qq and most modern texts = 'not'

W [3] F1 shows no extra word, Qq and most modern texts = 'right'

5

In any case let Thisby have cleane linnen: and let not him
that playes the Lion, paire his nailes, for they shall hang
out for the Lions clawes.

And most deare Actors, eate
no Onions, nor Garlicke; for wee are to utter sweete
breath, and I doe not doubt but to heare them say, it is a
sweet Comedy.

No more words: away, go away.

[Exeunt]

Actus Quintus

ENTER THESEUS, HIPPOLITA, EGEUS [1] AND HIS LORDS

Hippolita	'Tis strange my Theseus, ÿ [2] these lovers speake of.
Theseus	More strange then true.

        I never may beleeve
These anticke[3] fables, nor these Fairy toyes,
Lovers and mad men have such seething braines,

> Such shaping phantasies, that apprehend more/ [4]
> Then coole reason ever comprehends.
>
> The Lunaticke/, the Lover, and the Poet,
> Are of imagination all compact/.

One sees more divels then vaste hell can hold;
That is the mad man.
        The Lover, all as franticke,
Sees Helens beauty in a brow of Egipt.

> The Poets eye in a fine frenzy rolling,° doth glance
> From heaven to earth, from earth to heaven. °
>
> And as imagination bodies forth° the forms of things
> Unknowne; the Poets pen° turnes them to shapes,
> And gives to aire[5] nothing,° a locall habitation,
> And a name. °
>   Such tricks hath strong imagination,° [6]   159-c

[P][1] Qq present this character as Philostrate: however F1 reassigns nearly all his lines to Hermia's father, Egeus (see footnote #3, page 70): modern texts are divided as to whether they give the entry and lines to Qq's Philostrate or to F1's Egeus: (for further details, see the Specific Introduction to this play)

[AB][2] F1 = 'ÿ', (printed as such because of lack of column width), F2/most modern texts = that

[W][3] F1/Q2 = 'anticke', Q1 and most modern texts = 'antique'

[LS][4] some modern texts put the word 'more' at the start of the next line, thus reducing Theseus' beginning-to-get-excited, slightly irregular, two lines (9/11 syllables) to normal poetry (Q1's offering here of 11/13 and 7 syllables - as shown by the symbol / - is not reproduced in Q2/F1 and hardly ever shown in modern texts)

[W][5] F1 = 'aire', Qq and most modern texts = 'ayery'

[LS][6] save for Q1's placing of 'And as' at the end of a line instead of starting a new one, the F setting follows Q1 exactly: the irregular passage (13/8 - 10/14/10/12 or 13/12 or 13 syllables) shows Theseus struggling to express himself in matters we have never heard him attempt to talk of before in a brand new situation where, for the first time in the play, Hippolita has initiated the conversation: the modern texts' poetical restructuring (11/10 - 12/10/10/10 or 11/10/9 or 10) smoothes away both awkwardness and excitement, creating somewhat bland posturing where half-formed new concepts originally existed

That if it would but apprehend some joy,
It comprehends some bringer of that joy.
Or in the night, imagining some feare,
How easie is a bush suppos'd a Beare?

Hippolita   But all the storie of the night told over,
And all their minds transfigur'd so together,
More witnesseth than fancies images,
And growes to something of great constancie;
But howsoever, strange, and admirable.

**ENTER LOVERS, LYSANDER, DEMETRIUS, HERMIA,
AND HELENA**

Theseus   Heere come the lovers, full of joy and mirth:
Joy, gentle friends, joy and fresh dayes
Of love accompany your hearts.

Lysander   More then to us, ° waite in your royall walkes,
your boord, your bed.° [1]

Theseus   Come now, what maskes, what dances shall
we have,
To weare away this long age of three houres,
Between/ our after supper, and bed-time?

Where is our usuall manager/ of mirth?

What Revels are in hand?
Is there no play/, [2]

To ease the anguish of a torturing houre?

Call Egeus. [3]

Egeus   Heere mighty Theseus. ˘

Theseus   Say, what abridgement have you for this evening?
       What maske?
           What musicke?
               How shall we beguile
The lazie time, if not with some delight?

R 159 - c : 5.1.19 - 41

^{VP} 1
  F1/Qq allow a moment of awkward prose as Lysander touches on the idea of bed among other matters
    uppermost in all the lovers' minds: most modern texts alter the passage to verse, as the symbol ° shows
LS 2
  some modern texts follow Q1's much more erratic setting of Theseus' attempt to pass away the evening
    (12/16/12 syllables): other modern texts reproduce F1's pentameter (10/10/10/10)
P 3
  as noted above, some modern texts follow Qq's renaming this character Philostrate throughout Act Five

Egeus	There is a breefe how many sports are rife : Make choise of which your Highnesse will see first .
Lis ¹	*The battell with the Centaurs to be sung* *By an Athenian Eunuch, to the Harpe .*
Theseus	Wee'l none of that. That have I told my Love In glory of my kinsman Hercules .
Lis	*The riot of the tipsie Bachanals,* *Tearing the Thracian singer, in their rage?*
Theseus	That is an old device, and it was plaid When I from Thebes came last a Conqueror .
Lis	*The thrice three Muses, mourning for the death* *of ² learning, late deceast in beggerie .*
Theseus	That is some Satire keene and criticall, Not sorting with a nuptiall ceremonie .
Lis	*A tedious breefe Scene of yong Piramus,* *And his love Thisby ; very tragicall mirth .*

Theseus	Merry and tragicall?
	       Tedious, and briefe? °
	               That
	is, hot ice/, and wondrous strange snow. °
	            How shall wee
	finde the concord /of this discord? ° ³

Egeus	A play there is, my Lord, some ten words long, Which is as breefe, as I have knowne a play ; But by ten words, my Lord, it is too long ; Which makes it tedious. For in all the play, There is not one word apt, one Player fitted .

SD/P/STRUCT ₁
   all modern texts add a stage direction that Egeus (or Philostrate) has handed a list to Theseus: however, the prefix that now appears causes a problem as to who actually reads what: Qq print one prefix 'The.' just before the line 'The battell with . . . ' and thus Theseus reads the complete 'breefe': F1 prints the prefix 'The.' every time Theseus makes a comment on the 'breefe' and a second prefix 'Lis.' every time the offerings of the 'breefe' are read: some modern texts assume that it is Egeus (or Philostrate) who reads, others assume this to be Lysander; some assume that it simply refers to the 'List' of suggested entertainments and make no reference as to who reads it out aloud, and accordingly some productions have the list passed among all the Lovers, with each one of them reading part of it aloud: this script will simply print 'Lis' when it appears in F1 and allow each reader/actor/director to make their own decision - (the prefix 'Lis.' will be bolded to separate it from what is being read from the paper): for clarity the titles of the various offerings are set in italics, not an F1 practice

VP ₂
Ff set 'of' as if it started a line of prose, Qq and most modern texts = 'Of'

VP ₃
Q2/F1 print this passage as prose, Q1 in a peculiar verse form (13/13/4 syllables as shown by /): most modern texts restructure the speech into more regular verse (10/9/11), as the symbols ° show

And tragicall my noble Lord it is : ° for Piramus
Therein doth kill himselfe. °
                    Which when I saw
Rehearst, I must confesse,° made mine eyes water :
But more merrie teares,° the passion of loud laughter
Never shed. °

Theseus   What are they that do play it? [}] ¹

Egeus   Hard handed men, that worke in Athens heere,
Which never labour'd in their mindes till now;
And now have toyled their unbreathed memories
With this same play, against your nuptiall.

Theseus   And we will heare it.   R 159 - c

Philostrate ²   No, my noble Lord, °it is not for you.
                    I have heard
It over,° and it is nothing, nothing in the world; °

Unlesse you can finde sport in their intents,
Extreamely strecht, and cond with cruell paine,

To doe you service.

Theseus   I will heare that play. °
                    For never any thing
Can be amisse,° when simplenesse and duty tender it.° ³

Goe bring them in, ⁴ and take your places, Ladies.

Hippolita   I love not to see wretchednesse orecharged;
And duty in his service perishing.

Theseus   Why gentle sweet, you shall see no such thing.

Hippolita   He saies, they can doe nothing in this kinde.

R 159 - c / L 160 - c : 5.1.66 - 88

^{LS} 1
the F1/Qq layout (14/10/11/12/10 as a split line) allows Egeus/Philostrate wonderful lack of self-control,
  especially on the opening line, as he describes the aesthetic horrors of the piece: the modern restructuring
  to regular poetry (10/10/10/10/10/7) completely destroys this

^{PLS} 2
for the only time in F1, the prefix Philostrate appears in Act Five: most modern texts who have altered
  Philostrate to Egeus throughout ignore this and alter the prefix to 'Ege.' denying Philostrate any place in
  the remainder of the play: however, it may be rather splendid to have him come on with the courtiers at
  the top of the scene and here allow his one overbearing personal revue: whoever gets the lines, the F1/Qq
  imbalance (a 5 syllable statement from Theseus followed by a momentary pause, and then two explosive
  13 syllable lines) is more theatrically interesting than the poetic revamping (11/10/10) of the modern texts

^{LS} 3
again the modern revamping to poetry (10 syllables as a split line/10/10) totally destroys the F1/Qq's
  very firm and decisive build for Thescus, a pause after Philostrate/Egeus's 5 syllable short line and then
  an 11/14 syllable final self assertion.

^{SD} 4
most modern texts add a stage direction here for someone to go and fetch the Mechanicals

Theseus	The kinder we, to give them thanks for nothing[1]
	Our sport shall be, to take what they mistake;

> And what poore duty cannot doe,° noble respect
> Takes it in might, not merit.° [2]

10 Where I have come, great Clearkes have purposed
    To greete me with premeditated welcomes;
    Where I have seene them shiver and looke pale,
    Make periods in the midst of sentences,
    Throttle their practiz'd accent in their feares,
15 And in conclusion, dumbly have broke off,
    Not paying me a welcome.
                              Trust me sweete,
    Out of this silence yet, I pickt a welcome:
    And in the modesty of fearefull duty,
20 I read as much, as from the ratling tongue
    Of saucy and audacious eloquence.

    Love therefore, and tongue-tide simplicity,
    In least, speake most, to my capacity. [3]

Egeus	So please your Grace, the Prologue is addrest.
Theseus as 25 **Duke** [4]	Let him approach.

[Flor{ish} Trum{pets}]
ENTER THE PROLOGUE {Quince}

{Quince as} **Prologue**

    If we offend, it is with our good will.

    That you should thinke, we come not to offend,
    But with good will.
                To shew our simple skill,
30   That is the true beginning of our end.

    Consider then, we come but in despight.

    We do not come, as minding to content you,
    Our true intent is.
                All for your delight,
35   We are not heere.
                That you should here repent you,

RCT [1] Qq/F4/most modern texts set a period, F2-3 a colon: F1 sets no punctuation as if Theseus hurries on
with his explanation of 'noblesse oblige'

LS [2] F1/Qq give Theseus a moment of extra persuasion (12 syllables) and a moment of respite (7, during
which silence Hippolita might tacitly concur): modern texts revamp his passion yet again into more regular
poetry (8, sometimes expanded to 10 with the addition of a word such as 'willingly'/10)

SD [3] most modern texts add a stage direction that Quince (either alone or with all the Mechanicals) appears

P [4] as the Prologue approaches, Theseus is (momentarily) given the prefix of Duke in both F1/Qq for the
first time in the play, a wonderful potential acting note: see also footnote #3, page 77

The Actors are at hand; and by their show,
You shall know all, that you are like to know . [1]

· Theseus ·   This fellow doth not stand upon points .

Lysander   He hath rid his[2] Prologue, like a rough Colt : he
knowes not the stop .
                        A good morall my Lord .
                                    It is not
enough to speake, but to speake true .

Hippolita   Indeed hee hath plaid on his Prologue, like a
childe on a Recorder, a sound, but not in government .

Theseus   His speech was like a tangled chaine : nothing
impaired, but all disordered .
                            Who is next?

TAWYER [3] WITH A TRUMPET BEFORE THEM
ENTER PYRAMUS AND THISBY, WALL, MOONE-SHINE, AND LYON

{Quince as} **Prologue**

Gentles, perchance you wonder at this show,
But wonder on, till truth make all things plaine.

This man is Piramus, if you would know;
This beauteous Lady, Thisby is certaine .

This man, with lyme and rough-cast, doth present
Wall, that vile wall, which did these lovers sunder :
And through walls chink (poor soules) they are content
To whisper .
                At the which, let no man wonder .

This man, with Lanthorne, dog, and bush of thorne,
Presenteth moone-shine .
                       For if you will know,
By moone-shine did these Lovers thinke no scorne
To meet at Ninus toombe, there, there to wooe :   L 160 - c
This grizy[4] beast (which Lyon hight by name)
The trusty Thisby, comming first by night,
Did scarre away, or rather did affright :
And as she fled, her mantle she did fall;
Which Lyon vile with bloody mouth did staine .

L 160 - c / R 160 - c : 5.1.116 - 143

SD [1] most modern texts add a stage direction for Quince to exit, but this is not necessary - especially if the others came in with him: what he is probably required to do is draw away from the noble audience

W [2] F1/Q1 = 'his', Q2 and most modern texts = 'this'

F/P [3] Tawyer was manservant to Heminge, one of the principal actors (also a share-holder of the company, and who with Condell was a prime instigator in providing the material for the First Folio)

W [4] F1 = 'grizy', F2/Qq and most modern texts = 'grizzly'

Anon comes Piramus, sweet youth and tall,
And findes his Thisbies Mantle slaine;
Whereat, with blade, with bloody blamefull blade,
He bravely broacht his boiling bloudy breast,
And Thisby, tarrying in Mulberry shade,
His dagger drew, and died.
                          For all the rest,
Let Lyon, Moone-shine, Wall, and Lovers twaine,
At large discourse, while here they doe remaine.

EXIT ALL BUT WALL [1]

Theseus   I wonder if the Lion be to speake.

Demetrius   No wonder, my Lord: one Lion may, when
                     many Asses doe.

EXIT LYON, THISBIE, AND MOONESHINE [2]

{Snout as} **Wall**

In this same Interlude, it doth befall,
That I, one Snowt (by name) present a wall:
And such a wall, as I would have you thinke,
That had in it a crannied hole or chinke:
Through which the Lovers, Piramus and Thisbie
Did whisper often, very secretly.

This loame, this rough-cast, and this stone doth shew,
That I am that same Wall; the truth is so.

And this the cranny is, right and sinister,
Through which the fearefull Lovers are to whisper.

Theseus   Would you desire Lime and Haire to speake
                     better?

Demetrius   It is the wittiest partition, that ever I heard
                     discourse, my Lord.

Theseus   Pyramus drawes neere the Wall, silence.

ENTER PYRAMUS

R 160 - c : 5.1.144 - 169

[SD 1] the instructions inherent in this stage direction seem to be repeated in a different way in just three lines (see next footnote): however, if all the characters except Snout/Wall withdraw just from the direct attention of the watching Court, then both stage directions can apply: (this direction does not appear in Q1 but is printed in most modern texts)

[SD 2] if this direction is allowed to stay as well as the one three lines earlier (see footnote above), then Snout (already on stage) Piramus and Thisby can still remain just beyond the Court's direct attention while the others leave the stage completely; (though this stage direction does appear in Q1 most modern texts do not print it)

{Bottome as} **Piramus**

> O grim lookt night, ô night with hue so blacke,
> O night, which ever art, when day is not:
> O night, ô night, alacke, alacke, alacke,
> I feare my Thisbies promise is forgot.

> And thou ô wall, thou sweet and lovely wall, [1]
> That stands[2] betweene her fathers ground and mine,
> Thou wall, ô wall, ô sweet and lovely wall,
> Shew me thy chinke, to blinke through with mine eine . [3]

> Thankes courteous wall.
> > > Jove shield thee well for this.

> But what see I?
> > > No Thisbie doe I see.

> O wicked wall, through whom I see no blisse.

> Curst be thy stones for thus deceiving mee.

Theseus

The wall me-thinkes being sensible, should
curse againe.

Piramus [4] No in truth sir, he should not.
> > Deceiving me,
> Is Thisbies cue; she is to enter,[5] and I am to spy
> Her through the wall.
> > > You shall see it will fall.

ENTER THISBIE

Pat as I told you; yonder she comes.

{Flute as} **Thisby**

> O wall, full often hast thou heard my mones,
> For parting my faire Piramus, and me.

> My cherry lips have often kist thy stones;
> Thy stones with Lime and Haire knit up in thee.

{Bottome as} **Piramus**

> I see a voyce; now will I to the chinke,
> To spy and I can heare my Thisbies face.
> > > Thisbie? [6]

[W1] F1 = 'thou sweet and lovely wall', Qq and most modern texts = 'o sweet, o lovely wall'

[W2] F1/Q2 = 'stands', Q1 and most modern texts = 'standst'

[SD3] most modern texts add a stage direction for Snout somehow to offer Bottome a chink to peer through

[VP4] though F1/Qq print this as the only verse speech Bottome makes, except when playing Piramus, by printing the verse as prose most modern texts remove his attempted delicacy in a doubly difficult situation (a theatrical mess-up and talking to his social superiors): notice his prefix stays in character

[W5] F1/Q2 print no extra word, Q1 and most modern texts = 'now'

[LS6] though Qq/Ff keep the final 'Thisbie' as part of a twelve syllable line, most modern texts set it on a separate line, creating a pause where none originally existed

{Flute as} **Thisby**

25   My Love thou art, my Love I thinke.

{Bottome as} **Piramus**

Thinke what thou wilt, I am thy Lovers grace,
And like Limander am I trusty still.

{Flute as} **Thisby**

And I like Helen till the Fates me kill.

{Bottome as} **Piramus**

Not Shafalus to Procrus, was so true.

{Flute as} **Thisby**

30   As Shafalus to Procrus, I to you.   R 160 - c

{Bottome as} **Piramus**

O kisse me through the hole of this vile wall. ¹

{Flute as} **Thisby**

I kisse the wals hole, not your lips at all.

{Bottome as} **Piramus**

Wilt thou at Ninnies tombe meete me straight
way?

{Flute as} **Thisby**

35   Tide life, tide death, I come without delay.

{Snout as} **Wall**

Thus have I Wall, my part discharged so ;
And being done, thus Wall away doth go .

[Exit Clow] ²

Theseus as
Duke ³   Now is the morall downe ⁴ between the two
                    Neighbors.

240   **Demetrius**   No remedie my Lord, when Wals are so wil-
                    full, to heare⁵ without warning.

R 160 - c / L 163* - b : 5.1.195 - 209

^{SD}₁ most modern texts explain that in attempting to kiss Bottome/Piramus Flute/Thisbe kisses Snout/Wall's
fingers instead

^{SD}₂ it is not clear whether this stage direction is singular, referring just to Snout/Wall, or plural, referring to
Bottome/Piramus and Flute/Thisby too, consequently some modern texts take Bottome and Flute out as
soon as they finish speaking, while others let them wait and have all three exit when Snout finishes

^P₃ for the second time in the play Theseus' prefix changes to 'Du.' in F1 and 'Duk.' in Q1 (both shorthand
for Duke): possibly whatever he and the others feel about the entertainment requires some change of
behaviour in him - perhaps along the lines of his advice given to Hippolita earlier, page 73, concerning
the responsibility of great ones

^W₄ Ff = 'murall downe', Qq = 'moon used' (which no commentator has been able to explain satisfactorily),
some modern texts = 'wall down'

^W₅ though most modern texts agree with Ff/Qq and print this as 'heare ': one interesting gloss = 'leave'

Hippolita as **Dutchess** [1]	This is the silliest stuffe that ere[2] I heard.
Duke	The best in this kind are but shadowes, and the worst are no worse, if imagination amend them.
Dutchess	It must be your imagination then, & not theirs.
Duke	If wee imagine no worse of them then they of themselves, they may passe for excellent men.

Here com

two noble beasts, in[3] a man and a Lion.

ENTER LYON AND MOONE-SHINE [4]

{Snug as} **Lyon**

You Ladies, you (whose gentle harts do feare
The smallest monstrous mouse that creepes on floore)
May now perchance, both quake and tremble heere,
When Lion rough in wildest rage doth roare.

Then know that I, one[5] Snug the Joyner am
A Lion fell, nor else no Lions dam:
For if I should as Lion come in strife
Into this place, 'twere pittie of[6] my life.

Duke	A verie gentle beast, and of a good conscience.
Demetrius	The verie best at a beast, my Lord, ÿ[7] ere I saw.
Lysander	This Lion is a verie Fox for his valor.
Duke	True, and a Goose for his discretion.
Demetrius	Not so my Lord: for his valor cannot carrie his discretion, and the Fox carries the Goose.
Duke	His discretion I am sure cannot carrie his valor: for the Goose carries not the Fox.

It is well; leave it to

his discretion, and let us hearken[8] to the Moone.

L 163* - b : 5.1.210 - 238

[P 1] now, as if following Theseus' example, Hippolita's prefix alters to 'Dut:'. in F1 and 'Dutch:' in Q1 (both shorthand for Dutchess): if so, perhaps some of the apparent sting of her lines might be mollified

[W 2] F1/Q2 = 'ere', Q1 and most modern texts = 'ever'

[PCT 3] some modern texts repunctuate F1/Qq's 'two noble beasts, in a man and a Lion.' to two noble beasts in, a man and a Lion.'

[SD 4] most modern texts list the props Moone-shine mentions, his dog, his bush, and - above all - his lantern

[W 5] F1 = 'one', Qq and most modern texts = 'as'

[W 6] F1 = 'of', Qq and most modern texts = 'on'

[AB 7] F1 = 'ÿ', (printed as such because of lack of column width), F2/most modern texts = 'that'

[W 8] F1/Q2 = 'hearken', Q1 and most modern texts = 'listen'

{Starveling as} **Moone**
>This Lanthorne doth the horned Moone pre-
>sent.

Demetrius　He should have worne the hornes on his head.

Duke　Hee is no crescent, and his hornes are invisible,
within the circumference.

{Starveling as} **Moone**
>This lanthorne doth the horned Moone pre-
>sent: ° My selfe, the man i'th Moone doth seeme to be. ° 1

Duke　This is the greatest error of all in the rest; the
man should be put into the Lanthorne.
>How is it els the man

i'th Moone?

Demetrius　He dares not come there for the candle. ²

>For you see, it is already in snuffe. ³

Dutchess　I am wearie⁴ of this Moone; would he would
change.

Duke　It appeares by his smal light of discretion, that
he is in the wane: but yet in courtesie, in all reason, we
must stay the time.

Lysander　Proceed Moone.

{Starveling as} **Moone**
>All that I have to say, is to tell you, that the
>Lanthorne is the Moone; I, the man in the⁵ Moone; this
>thorne bush, my thorne bush; and this dog, my dog.

Demetrius　Why all these should be in the Lanthorne: for
they⁶ are in the Moone.
>But silence, heere comes Thisby.

ENTER THISBY

{Flute as} **Thisby**
>This is old Ninnies tombe: where is my love?

L 163* - b : 5.1.239 - 263

VP 1 though F1 shows it as prose, Qq and most modern texts print the passage as verse

PCT 2 F4/most modern texts set a semi-colon: Qq/F1-3 set a period

VP 3 F1 suggests this is verse even though Qq and most modern texts print this as prose

W 4 F1/Q2 = 'wearie', Q1 and most modern texts = 'aweary'

W 5 F1 = 'in the', Qq and most modern texts = 'i'th'

W 6 F1/Q2 = 'for they', Q1 and most modern texts = 'for all these'

{Snug as} **Lyon**
     Ch.

[The Lion roares, Thisby runs off] [1]

95	**Demetrius**	Well roar'd Lion.

L 163[2] - b

Duke	Well run Thisby.
Dutchess	Well shone Moone.
	Truly the Moone shines with a good grace. [3]
Duke	Wel mouz'd Lion.
00 **Demetrius**	And then came Piramus.
Lysander	And so the Lion vanisht.

[4] **ENTER PIRAMUS**

{Bottome as} **Piramus**
     Sweet Moone, I thank thee for thy sunny beames,
     I thanke thee Moone, for shining now so bright:
     For by thy gracious, golden, glittering beames, [5]
05 I trust to taste [6] of truest Thisbies [7] sight.

     But stay: O spight! ° but marke, poore Knight,°
     What dreadfull dole is heere? °

     Eyes do you see ! °
             How can it be! °

10 O dainty Ducke: O Deere !

     Thy mantle good ; ° what staind with blood ! °

     Approch you [8] Furies fell : °
     O Fates ! come, come : ° Cut thred and thrum, °

L 163* - b / R 163* - b : 5.1.264 - 287

SD 1
  most modern texts explain that in running away, Flute/Thisby drops a handkerchief which Snug/Lion 'bloodies'

COMP 2
  F1 numbers this page incorrectly: in accurate numerical sequence this should be numbered as L161

VP 3
  Qq/most modern texts set this as prose: Ff sets it as two verse lines, perhaps suggesting Hippolita is
  now attempting as the Dutchess (now her given prefix) to smooth Starveling/ Moone's hurt feelings

SD 4
  modern texts offer various combinations of stage directions to give Snug/Lyon an exit prior to the entry
  of Bottome/Piramus: the placing of the F1/Qq entry is splendid, for one reading could be that the Court
  might have to give Snug/Lyon the hint to leave the stage before Bottome/Piramus will deign to come on

W/ALT 5
  F1/Qq = 'beames', most modern texts = 'gleams' (to preserve the alliterative quality of the line -
  though, of course, in not keeping to it, Bottome may have momentarily forgotten the correct word): also
  what is quite peculiar, here the modern texts alter the word to create alliteration, but in the very next line
  (see the following footnote) they go back to Qq and destroy Ff's alliteration of 'trust/taste/truest'

W 6
  F1 = 'taste', Qq and most modern texts = 'take'

W 7
  F1 = 'Thisbies', Qq and most modern texts = 'Thisby'

W 8
  F1 = 'you', Qq and most modern texts = 'ye'

	Quaile, crush, conclude, and quell . [1]

Duke
This passion, and the death of a deare friend,
Would go neere to make a man looke sad. [2]

Dutchess
Beshrew my heart, but I pittie the man.

{Bottome as} **Piramus**
O wherefore Nature, did'st thou Lions frame?
Since Lion vilde hath heere deflour'd my deere:
Which is: no, no, which was the fairest Dame
That liv'd, that lov'd, that lik'd, that look'd with cheere.

Come teares, confound: ° Out sword, and wound°
The pap of Piramus: °
I, that left pap,° where heart doth hop; °
Thus dye I, thus, thus, thus. ° [3]

Now am I dead,° now am I fled,° my soule is in the sky,°
Tongue lose thy light,° Moone take thy flight,° [4]
Now dye, dye, dye, dye, dye. [5] [6]

Demetrius
No Die, but an ace for him; for he is but one.

Lysander
Lesse then an ace man.
For he is dead, he is no-
thing.

Duke
With the helpe of a Surgeon, he might yet reco-
ver, and prove an Asse.

Dutchess
How chance Moone-shine is gone before?
Thisby comes backe, and findes her Lover.

ENTER THISBY [7]

R 163* · b : 5.1.288 - 313

LS [1]
as Quince suggested in Act Three Scene, 1 he has finally written a passage with lines alternating in
syllable length of 'eight and six' (though not the Prologue he promised for Bottome) and this is how F1/Qq
print it: despite this, most modern texts reproduce the section according to its rhyme scheme as the
symbols ° show, and the extra line breaks so caused create an entirely different rhythm for the speaker
than the source text suggests (see also footnotes #6, below and #6, page 82 and the specific introduction)

VP [2]
while the idea of Theseus being moved to verse by Bottome is very interesting, only Ff print it as such

SD [3]
most modern texts add a stage direction that here Bottome/Piramus begins to stab himself

SD [4]
most modern texts add a stage direction for Starveling/Moone-shine to exit at any point between now
and Hippolita's next speech in six lines time

SD [5]
most modern texts add a stage direction that, at last, Bottome/Piramus finally 'dies'

LS [6]
again, most modern texts have taken F1/Qq's 'eight and six' and printed according to rhyme rather than
the archaic verse pattern it is supposed to represent: see footnote #1 above, and the whole of Thisby's
final speech on the next page

SD [7]
some modern texts delay Thisby's entry for a line: though logical, it is not very theatrical, for Flute could
enter too soon (as Ff suggest) and have to wait until Theseus finishes: (Qq do not specify Thisby's entry)

Duke	She wil finde him by starre-light.
	Heere she comes, and her passion ends the play.
Dutchess	Me thinkes shee should not use a long one for
340	such a Piramus: I hope she will be breefe.
Demetrius	A Moth[1] wil turne the ballance, which Piramus
	which Thisby is the better. [2]
Lysander	She hath spyed him already, with those sweete eyes. †
Demetrius	And thus she meanes, *videlicit*.

{Flute as} **Thisby**

345   Asleepe my Love?°

        What, dead my Dove? °

   O Piramus arise: °

   Speake, Speake.

        Quite dumbe?°

350   Dead, dead?

           A tombe°

   Must cover thy sweet eyes. °

   These Lilly Lips,° this cherry nose,°

   These yellow Cowslip cheekes°

355   Are gone, are gone: ° Lovers make mone: °

   His eyes were greene as Leekes. °

   O sisters three,° come, come to mee,°

   With hands as pale as Milke,°

   Lay them in gore,° since you have shore°

360   With sheeres, his thred of silke. °

   Tongue not a word: ° Come trusty sword: °

   Come blade, my brest imbrue: ° [3]   R 163[4] - b

   And farwell friends,° thus Thisbie ends; °

   Adieu, adieu, adieu. ° [5] [6]

---

365 **Duke**	[7] Moon-shine & Lion are left to burie the dead.
Demetrius	I, and Wall too.

R 163* - b / L 162 - c : 5.1.314 - 350

W [1]
F1/Qq = 'Moth', most modern texts = 'Mote'

ADD/PCT [2]
   most modern texts alter the period to a colon and add the Qq words omitted by F1, 'he for a man;
God warnd [warrant] us; she, for a woman; God blesse us.'

SD [3]
   most modern texts add a stage direction that Flute/Thisby stabs him/herself

COMP [4]
   F1 numbers this page incorrectly: in strict sequence the column should be R161 (see footnote #2, p.80)

SD [5]
   most modern texts add the direction that Flute/Thisby now dies

LS [6]
   once again, most modern texts have taken F1/Qq's 'eight and six' and printed it according to rhyme
rather than the archaic verse pattern it is supposed to represent

SD [7]
   most modern texts add a conflicting variety of stage directions as to whether the 'dead' bodies wake
up or are removed, and as to what applause and bows are made: no indications are given in F/Qq

Bottome [1]   No, I assure you, the wall is downe, that parted
their Fathers.
370   Will it please you to see the Epilogue, or
to heare a Bergomask dance, betweene two of our company?

Duke   No Epilogue, I pray you; for your play needs
no excuse.
375   Never excuse; for when the plaiers are all
dcad, there need none to be blamed.
Marry, if hee that
writ it had plaid Piramus, and hung[2] himselfe in Thisbies
garter, it would have beene a fine Tragedy: and so it is
truely, and very notably discharg'd.
380   But come, your
Burgomaske; let your Epilogue alone.

[3]   The iron tongue of midnight hath told twelve.

Lovers to bed, 'tis almost Fairy time.

I feare we shall out-sleepe the comming morne,
385   As much as we this night have over-watcht.

This palpable grosse play hath well beguil'd
The heavy gate[4] of night.
Sweet friends to bed.

A fortnight hold we this solemnity.

390   In nightly Revels; and new jollitie.

[Exeunt]
ENTER PUCKE [5] [6]

P 1
quite delightfully, Q1 assigns this to the hitherto tongue-tied Snug as Lyon: Q2/F1 do not do so, and
all modern texts follow F1/Q2 in giving it to Bottome, arguing the speaking style could 'only' be his

W 2
F1 = 'hung', Qq and most modern texts = 'hangd'

SD 3
most modern texts add one stage direction for the Burgomaske (many productions ignoring the number
of 'two of our company' spoken of by Bottome - or Snug in Q1), and a second for one of the palace clocks
to strike midnight at the end (or during the last moments) of the dance

W 4
F1/Qq = gate, most modern texts = gait

SD 5
since Pucke/Robin refers to a broom at the end of his speech, nearly all modern texts have him bring
one in

ALT 6
some modern texts start a new scene here, Act Five Scene 2

Robin as
Pucke

1 Now the hungry Lyons [2] rores,
And the Wolfe beholds [3] the Moone :
Whilest the heavy ploughman snores,
All with weary taske fore-done .

95　Now the wasted brands doe glow,
Whil'st the scritch-owle, scritching loud,
Puts the wretch that lies in woe,
In remembrance of a shrowd .

100　Now it is the time of night,
That the graves, all gaping wide,
Every one lets forth his spright,
In the Church-way paths to glide . [4]

And we Fairies, that do runne,
By the triple Hecates teame,
105　From the presence of the Sunne,
Following darkenesse like a dreame,
Now are frollicke ; not a Mouse
Shall disturbe this hallowed house .

I am sent with broome before,
110　To sweep the dust behinde the doore .

ENTER KING AND QUEENE OF FAIRIES, WITH THEIR TRAINE

Oberon　Through the house give glimmering light,　L 162 - c
By the dead and drowsie fier,
Everie Elfe and Fairie spright,
Hop as light as bird from brier,
415　And this Ditty after me,° 　sing and dance it trippinglie . ° [5]

Titania　First rehearse this[6] song by roate,
To each word a warbling note .

Hand in hand, with Fairie grace,
Will we sing and blesse this place .

M [1] for the first time in the play Pucke/Robin is able to complete a magic/ritual speech without any break
in the pattern

W [2] F1/Qq = 'Lyons', most modern texts = 'lion'

W [3] F1/Qq = 'beholds', most modern texts = 'behowls'

PCT [4] F1 sets a somewhat indistinct period, F2-4 a comma: most modern texts set a period or colon

MLS [5] as Oberon is about to direct the Fairies to the various tasks they must perform to complete the blessing,
F1/Qq show the line as a double length line of magic: most modern texts split the line in two, as shown

W [6] F1/Q2 = 'this', Q1 and most modern texts = 'your' (choice here is not merely a matter of semantics:
either is possible, but the final choice will have a specific - and different - impact as to how the action
of the song will be staged)

THE SONG [1]

[2] *Now untill the breake of day,*
Through this house each Fairy stray .

To the best Bride-bed will we,
Which by us shall blessed be :
And the issue there create,
Ever shall be fortunate :
So shall all the couples three,
Ever true in loving be :
And the blots of Natures hand,
Shall not in their issue stand .

Never mole, harelip, nor scarre,
Nor marke prodigious, such as are
Despised in Nativitie, [3]
Shall upon their children be .

With this field dew consecrate,
Every Fairy take his gate , [4]
And each severall chamber blesse,
Through this Pallace with sweet peace,

Ever shall in safety rest,
And the owner of it blest . [5]

Trip away, make no stay ; [6]
Meet me all by breake of day . [7]

· **Robin** · [8]

If we shadowes have offended,
Thinke but this (and all is mended)
That you have but slumbred heere,
While these visions did appeare .

And this weake and idle theame,
No more yeelding but a dreame,
Gentles, [9] **doe not reprehend .**

[SD 1] most modern texts alter the stage direction for them all to dance as well as sing

[SPD 2] most modern texts do not consider this to be the text of the song, but treat it as a separate speech
when the song and dance are completed and, following Qq, they assign the speech to Oberon: however,
the F1 layout prints the text in italics showing that this is the song that Titania has said she will teach them:
as earlier (pages 23-4 this text) most of the lines are in the magical/ritual pattern and will be bolded accordingly

[M 3] it is fascinating that as the serious afflictions are faced, the magic pattern is momentarily broken

[W 4] F1/Qq = 'gate', most modern texts = 'gait'

[ALT/LS 5] though printed this way in F1/Qq, most modern texts tend to reverse these two lines

[M 6] the magic pattern seems to break (just for one line) as the command to perform their various tasks is
given: it still could be spoken as magic if there were a momentary silent breath between the two phrases
(after 'away')

[SD 7] most modern texts add a stage direction here for all to exeunt except Robin/Pucke

[P 8] as the character faces the audience for the last time he switches back to his first guise, Robin

[W 9] F1 = 'Centles', F2/Qq/most modern texts = 'Gentles'

If you pardon, we will mend .

[1] And as I am an honest Pucke,
If we have unearned lucke,
Now to scape the Serpents tongue,
We will make amends ere long:
Else the Pucke a lyar call .

So good night unto you all .

[2] Give me your hands, if we be friends,
And Robin shall restore amends .

R 162 - c

450

455

FINIS

R 162 - c : 5.1.430 - 438

[M1] as he refers to his 'honesty', so the magic pattern of the speech slips for a moment
[M2] the pattern of the magic/ritual is dispensed with for the final couplet

APPENDIX A
THE UNEASY RELATIONSHIP OF FOLIO, QUARTOS, AND MODERN TEXTS

Between the years 1590 and 1611, one William Shakespeare, a playwright and actor, delivered to the company of which he was a major shareholder at least thirty-seven plays in handwritten manuscript form. Since the texts belonged to the company upon delivery, he derived no extra income from publishing them. Indeed, as far as scholars can establish, he took no interest in the publication of his plays.

Consequently, without his supervision, yet during his lifetime and shortly after, several different publishers printed eighteen of these plays, each in separate editions. Each of these texts, known as **'Quartos'** because of the page size and method of folding each printed sheet, was about the size of a modern hardback novel. In 1623, seven years after Shakespeare's death, Heminges and Condell, two friends, theatrical colleagues, actors, and fellow shareholders in the company, passed on to the printer, William Jaggard, the handwritten copies of not only these eighteen plays but a further eighteen, of which seventeen had been performed but not yet seen in print.[1] These thirty-six plays were issued in one large volume, each page about the size of a modern legal piece of paper. Anything printed in this larger format was known as 'folio', again because of the page size and the method of sheet folding. Thus the 1623 printing of the collected works is known as **the First Folio,** its 1632 reprint (with more than 1600 unauthorised corrections) the Second Folio, and the next reprint, the 1666 Third Folio, added the one missing play, *Pericles* (which had been set in quarto and performed).

The handwritten manuscript used for the copies of the texts from which both Quartos and the First Folio were printed came from a variety of sources. Closest to Shakespeare were those in his own hand, known as the 'foul papers' because of the natural blottings, crossings out, and corrections. Sometimes he had time to pass the material on to a manuscript copyist who would make a clean copy, known as the 'fair papers'. Whether fair (if there was sufficient time) or foul (if the performance deadline was close), the papers would be passed on to the Playhouse, where a 'Playhouse copy' would be made, from which the 'sides' (individual copies of each part with just a single cue line) would be prepared for each actor. Whether Playhouse copy, fair papers, or foul, the various Elizabethan and Jacobean handwritten manuscripts from which the quartos and Folio came have long since disappeared.

The first printed texts of the Shakespeare plays were products of a speaking-

---

[1]   Though written between 1605–09, *Timon of Athens* was not performed publicly until 1761.

hearing society. They were based on rhetoric, a verbal form of arranging logic and argument in a persuasive, pleasing, and entertaining fashion so as to win personal and public debates, a system which allowed individuals to express at one and the same time the steppingstones in an argument while releasing the underlying emotional feelings that accompanied it.[2] Naturally, when ideas were set on paper they mirrored this same form of progression in argument and the accompanying personal release, allowing both neat and untidy thoughts to be seen at a glance (see the General Introduction, pp. xvi–xxi). Thus what was set on paper was not just a silent debate. It was at the same time a reminder of how the human voice might be heard both logically and passionately in that debate.

Such reminders did not last into the eighteenth century. Three separate but interrelated needs insisted on cleaning up the original printings so that silent and speaking reader alike could more easily appreciate the beauties of one of England's greatest geniuses.

First, by 1700, publishing's main thrust was to provide texts to be read privately by people of taste and learning. Since grammar was now the foundation for all writing, publication, and reading, all the Elizabethan and early Jacobean material still based on rhetoric appeared at best archaic and at worst incomprehensible. All printing followed the new universality of grammatical and syntactical standards, standards which still apply today. Consequently any earlier book printed prior to the establishment of these standards had to be reshaped in order to be understood. And the Folio/Quarto scripts, even the revamped versions which had already begun to appear, presented problems in this regard, especially when dealing in the moments of messy human behaviour. Thus, while the first texts were reshaped according to the grammatical knowledge of the 1700s, much of the shaping of the rhetoric was (inadvertently) removed from the plays.

Secondly, the more Shakespeare came to be recognized as a literary poet rather than as a theatrical genius, the less the plays were likely to be considered as performance texts. Indeed plot lines of several of his plays were altered (or ignored) to satisfy the more refined tastes of the period. And the resultant demands for poetic and literary clarity, as well as those of grammar, altered the first printings even further.

Thirdly, scholars argued a need for revision of both Quarto and Folio texts because of 'interfering hands' (hands other than Shakespeare's) having had undue influence on the texts. No matter whether foul or fair papers or Playhouse copy, so the argument ran, several intermediaries would be involved between Shakespeare's writ-

---

[2] For an extraordinarily full analysis of the art of rhetoric, readers are guided to Sister Miriam Joseph, *Shakespeare's Use of the Arts of Language* (New York: Haffner Publishing Co., 1947). For a more theatrical overview, readers are directed to Bertram Joseph, *Acting Shakespeare* (New York: Theatre Arts Books, 1960). For an overview involving aspects of Ff/Qq, readers are immodestly recommended to Neil Freeman, *Shakespeare's First Texts*, op. cit.

ing of the plays and the printing of them. If the fair papers provided the source text, a copyist might add some peculiarities, as per the well documented Ralph Crane.[3] If the Playhouse copy was the source text, extra information, mainly stage directions, would have been added by someone other than Shakespeare, turning the play from a somewhat literary document into a performance text. Finally, while more than five different compositors were involved in setting the First Folio, five did the bulk of the printing house work: each would have their individual pattern of typesetting — compositor E being singled out as far weaker than the rest. Thus between Shakespeare and the printed text might lie the hand(s) of as few as one and as many as three other people, even more when more than one compositor set an individual play. Therefore critics argue because there is the chance of so much interference between Shakespearean intent and the first printings of the plays, the plays do not offer a stylistic whole, i.e., while the words themselves are less likely to be interfered with, their shapings, the material consistently altered in the early 1700s, are not that of a single hand, and thus cannot be relied upon.

These well-intentioned grammatical and poetic alterations may have introduced Shakespeare to a wider reading audience, but their unforeseen effect was to remove the Elizabethan flavour of argument and of character development (especially in the areas of stress and the resulting textual irregularities), thus watering down and removing literally thousands of rhetorical and theatrical clues that those first performance scripts contained. And it is from this period that the division between ancient and modern texts begins. As a gross generalisation, the first texts, the First Folio and the quartos, could be dubbed 'Shakespeare for the stage'; the second, revamped early 1700 texts 'Shakespeare for the page'.

And virtually all current editions are based on the page texts of the early 1700s. While the words of each play remain basically the same, what shapes them, their sentences, punctuation, spelling, capitalisation, and sometimes even line structure, is often altered, unwittingly destroying much of their practical theatrical value.

It is important to neither condemn the modern editions nor blindly accept the authority of the early stage texts as gospel. This is not a case of 'old texts good, so modern texts bad'. The modern texts are of great help in literary and historical research, especially as to the meanings of obscure words and phrases, and in explaining literary allusions and historical events. They offer guidance to alternative text readings made by reputed editors, plus sound grammatical readings of difficult pas-

---

[3]   Though not of the theatre (his principle work was to copy material for lawyers) Crane was involved in the preparation of at least five plays in the Folio, as well as two plays for Thomas Middleton. Scholars characterise his work as demonstrating regular and careful scene and act division, though he is criticised for his heavy use of punctuation and parentheses, apostrophes and hyphens, and 'massed entry' stage directions, i.e. where all the characters with entrances in the scene are listed in a single direction at the top of the scene irrespective of where they are supposed to enter.

sages and clarification of errors that appear in the first printings.[4] In short, they can give the starting point of the play's journey, an understanding of the story, and the conflict between characters within the story. But they can only go so far.

They cannot give you fully the conflict within each character, the very essence for the fullest understanding of the development and resolution of any Shakespeare play. Thanks to their rhetorical, theatrical base the old texts add this vital extra element. They illustrate with great clarity the 'ever-changing present' (see p. xvi in the General Introduction) in the intellectual and emotional life of each character; their passages of harmony and dysfunction, and transitions between such passages; the moments of their personal costs or rewards; and their sensual verbal dance of debate and release. In short, the old texts clearly demonstrate the essential elements of living, breathing, reacting humanity—especially in times of joyous or painful stress.

By presenting the information contained in the First Folio, together with modern restructurings, both tested against theatrical possibilities, these texts should go far in bridging the gap between the two different points of view.

---

[4]   For example, the peculiar phrase 'a Table of greene fields' assigned to Mistress Quickly in describing the death of Falstaffe, *Henry V* (Act Two, Scene 3), has been superbly diagnosed as a case of poor penmanship being badly transcribed: the modern texts wisely set 'a babbled of green fields' instead.

NEIL FREEMAN trained as an actor at the Bristol Old Vic Theatre School. He has acted and directed in England, Canada, and the USA. Currently he is an Head of Graduate Directing and Senior Acting Professor in the Professional Training Programme of the Department of Theatre, Film, and Creative Writing at the University of British Columbia. He also teaches regularly at the National Theatre School of Canada, Concordia University, Brigham Young University in both Provo and Hawaii, and is on the teaching faculty of professional workshops in Montreal, Toronto and Vancouver. He is associated with Shakespeare & Co. in Lenox; the Will Geer Theatre in Los Angeles; Bard on the Beach in Vancouver; Repercussion Theatre in Montreal; and has worked with the Stratford Festival, Canada, and Shakespeare Santa Cruz.

His ground breaking work in using the first printings of the Shakespeare texts in performance, on the rehearsal floor and in the classroom has lead to lectures at the Shakespeare Association of America and workshops at both the ATHE and VASTA, and grants/fellowships from the National Endowment of the Arts (USA), The Social Science and Humanities Research Council (Canada), and York University in Toronto.

His three collations of Shakespeare and music - *A Midsummer Nights Dream* (for three actors, chorus, and Orchestra); *If This Be Love* (for three actors, mezzo-soprano, and Orchestra); *The Four Seasons of Shakespeare and Vivaldi* (for two actors, violin soloist and Chamber Orchestra) - commissioned and performed by Bard On The Beach and The Vancouver Symphony Orchestra have been received with great public acclaim.

THE APPLAUSE FIRST FOLIO OF SHAKESPEARE

Prepared & Annotated by Neil Freeman

"NEIL FREEMAN IS HANDING YOU THE SAME TEXT THAT WILLIAM SHAKESPEARE HANDED HIS ACTORS...DESTINED TO BECOME A STANDARD TEXT IN SCHOOLS, UNIVERSITIES AND LIBRARIES." —Tina Packer, Artistic Director *Shakespeare & Company*

The publication of the complete FIRST FOLIO OF SHAKESPEARE with all 36 plays in modern type (and at a non-scholarly, affordable price) allows readers for the first time to ponder and marvel at Shakespeare in the raw — with a little authoritative help from Neil Freeman, who painstakingly prepared and annotated the text.

Specially designed with a stay-flat, full-color leatherette binding.

ISBN 1-155783-333-8

SOLILOQUY!

The Shakespeare Monologues
Edited by Michael Earley and Philippa Keil

At last, over 175 of Shakespeare's finest and most performable monologues taken from all 37 plays are here in two easy-to-use volumes (MEN and WOMEN). Selections travel the entire spectrum of the great dramatist's vision, from comedies and romances to tragedies, pathos and histories.

"Soliloquy is an excellent and comprehensive collection of Shakespeare's speeches. Not only are the monologues wide-ranging and varied, but they are superbly annotated. Each volume is prefaced by an informative and reassuring introduction, which explains the signals and signposts by which Shakespeare helps an actor on his journey through the text. It includes a very good explanation of blank verse, with excellent examples of irregularities which are specifically related to character and acting intentions. These two books are a must for any actor in search of a 'classical' audition piece."

ELIZABETH SMITH
Head of Voice & Speech
The Juilliard School

paper•MEN: ISBN 0-936839-78-3
WOMEN: ISBN 0-936839-79-1

THE ACTOR AND THE TEXT
by Cicely Berry

As voice director of the Royal Shakespeare
Company, Cicely Berry has worked with actors such
as Jeremy Irons, Derek Jacobi, Jonathan Pryce, Sinead
Cusack and Antony Sher. *The Actor and The Text*
brings Ms. Berry's methods of applying vocal pro-
duction skills within a text to the general public.

While this book focuses primarily on speaking
Shakespeare, Ms. Berry also includes the speaking of
some modern playwrights, such as Edward Bond.

As Ms. Berry describes her own volume in the
introduction:

" … this book is not simply about making the
voice sound more interesting. It is about getting
inside the words we use …It is about making the language organic, so that the words act as a spur to the
sound …"

paper•ISBN 1-155783-138-6

APPLAUSE

SHAKESPEARE'S FIRST TEXTS

by Neil Freeman

"THE ACTOR'S BEST CHAMPION OF THE
FOLIO"   —Kristin Linklater
                  author of *Freeing Shakespeare's Voice*

Neil Freeman provides students, scholars, theatre-lovers, and, most importantly, actors and direc-tors, with a highly readable, illuminating, and indis-pensable guide to William Shakespeare's own first quill-inscribed texts — SHAKESPEARE'S FIRST TEXTS.

Four hundred years later, most of the grammatical and typographical information conveyed by this rep-resentation in Elizabethan type by the first play com-positors has been lost. Or, rather, discarded, in order to conform to the new standards of usage. Granted, this permitted more readers access to Shakespeare's writing, but it also did away with some of Shakespeare himself.

ISBN 1-155783-335-4